Like Lions Learning To Roar

Like Lions Learning To Roar

Dharma Talks by Seon Master Daehaeng
English translation and editing by
Hanmaum International Culture Institute
Cover design by Su Yeon Park
Published by Hanmaum Publications

First edition, first printing: February 2020

© 2020 Hanmaum Seonwon Foundation
All rights reserved, including the right to reproduce this work in any form.

within Korea
tel: (031)470-3175 / fax: (031)470-3209
Outside Korea
tel: (82-31)470-3175 / fax: (82-31)470-3209
E-mail: onemind@hanmaum.org

ISBN 978-89-91857-59-9 (03220)

Cataloging In Publication(CIP) of the National Library of Korea: 2020001800
For further publishing details see: http://seoji.nl.go.kr/
Or the Korean Library Information System Network at
http://www.nl.go.kr/kolisnet

Like Lions Learning To Roar

What if everyone was another
part of yourself...

**Seon Master
Daehaeng**

hanmaum

Contents

8   Foreword

12 About Daehaeng Kun Sunim

20 **Dancing on the Whirlwind**

74 **Turning Dirt into Gold**

140 Glossary

A Great Being

Go forward leaving behind no traces of yourself.

Become a great being,

who refuses nothing,

and views all things positively.

Become a great being,

who unconditionally embraces everything,

free of ideas of getting rid of or holding on to,

who doesn't try to block what comes,

nor cling to what leaves.

Become a great being,

neither stained by the things of the world,

nor clutching at them.

Become a great being,

who is the most ordinary person,

yet also the most extraordinary.

Foreword

You have to meet the teacher halfway.

You just do. There's no way around it. You have to be struggling and working and trying to figure things out for yourself first. Then everything else can happen. You have to be making an effort to figure out your own path. Then if you're fortunate enough to meet a good teacher, what they have to share with you will unlock doors, windows, or even the entire universe.

Seon Master Daehaeng intimately understood this. She was kind of scary in the way that she would never tell you a second time to do something. Either you were ready for what she'd said, or you weren't, and there was no point in saying more.

But if you were ready, then what she had to say would often be the missing piece, some aspect that should have been obvious, but which you'd overlooked. Some deep habit of thought that you kept entertaining, even though you'd have clearly seen the problem if it had belonged to someone else.

In this way, Seon Master Daehaeng wasn't raising chickens or pigeons, she was trying to raise lions. Lions who would learn to find their own way in the world. Lions who would take the principles she was teaching, use them to grow and develop, and experience for themselves this "big oneness." Lions who could then be a light to everyone else.

In fact, it doesn't matter that much if you're doing things wrong; what matters is that you're trying. If you're trying, then all it takes will be a bit of guidance for you to find your way. You'll make some wrong turns, you'll have to start some things over, and there will probably be a few painful lessons along the way, but if you're making the effort, then those things will all fall away.

What happens is this: You'll be reading along, when you come to a line that you may have read a dozen times before, but all of a sudden, it clicks. You see it as if for the first time. You may even wonder if that line was really in the book you read before!

You may hear a line in a Dharma talk, but this time it hits you like thunder, and later you won't remember anything else from the talk. Just that one line. Perhaps it would be something like, "You have to search within yourself," or "Everything is something you've contributed towards, so don't blame others," or "All minds and my mind are one mind."

Each one of us has this bright, one mind within us, and through it we are connected to all the universe. But it's up to us to discover this connection. It's up to us to live in tune with one mind. We have to figure out how this plays out in our life. But we can. Each of us can do this. It takes work to put our understanding into practice, and it's not easy to overcome all the strange habits we've developed as we evolved to this point. But it's certainly possible.

If you were born as a human being, then you are entitled to understand this connection, and you have everything you need to live in tune with it.

So work at relying upon this inherent one mind, this bright light of yours. Let go of your own stubbornness and bring this light into your life. And step forward into the world unafraid, undaunted by anything, neither fearing what comes to you, nor clinging to what leaves.

Go forward like a lion who's learned to roar.

With palms together,
Hanmaum International Culture Institute

About Daehaeng Kun Sunim

Daehaeng *Kun Sunim*[1] (1927 - 2012) was a rare teacher in Korea: a female *Seon(Zen)*[2] master, a nun whose students also included monks, and a teacher who helped revitalize Korean Buddhism by dramatically increasing the participation of young people and men.

She broke out of traditional models of spiritual practice to teach in such a way that allowed anyone to practice and awaken, making laypeople a particular focus of her efforts. At the same time, she was a major force for the advancement of *Bhikkunis*,[3] heavily supporting traditional nuns' colleges as well as the modern Bhikkuni Council of Korea.

---

1. Sunim / Kun Sunim: Sunim is the respectful title of address for a Buddhist monk or nun in Korea, and Kun Sunim is the title given to outstanding nuns or monks.

2. Seon(禪)(Chan, Zen): Seon describes the unshakeable state where one has firm faith in their inherent foundation, their Buddha-nature, and so returns everything they encounter back to this fundamental mind. It also means letting go of "I," "me," and "mine" throughout one's daily life.

Born in Seoul, Korea, she awakened when she was around eight years old and spent the years that followed learning to put her understanding into practice. For years, she wandered the mountains of Korea, wearing ragged clothes and eating only what was at hand. Later, she explained that she hadn't been pursuing some type of asceticism; rather, she was just completely absorbed in entrusting everything to her fundamental *Buddha*[4] essence and observing how that affected her life.

Those years profoundly shaped Kun Sunim's later teaching style; she intimately knew the great potential, energy, and wisdom inherent within each of us, and recognized that most of the people she encountered suffered because they didn't realize

---

3. Bhikkunis: Female sunims who are fully ordained are called *Bhikkuni*(比丘尼) sunims, while male sunims who are fully ordained are called *Bhikku*(比丘) sunims. This can also be a polite way of indicating male or female sunims.

4. Buddha: In this text, "Buddha" is capitalized out of respect, because it represents the essence and function of the enlightened mind. "The Buddha" always refers to Sakyamuni Buddha.

this about themselves. Seeing clearly the great light in every individual, she taught people to rely upon this inherent foundation, and refused to teach anything that distracted from this most important truth.

Without any particular intention to do so, Daehaeng Kun Sunim demonstrated on a daily basis the freedom and ability that arise when we truly connect with this fundamental essence inherent within us.

The sense of acceptance and connection people felt from being around her, as well as the abilities she manifested, weren't things she was trying to show off. In fact, she usually tried to hide them because people would tend to cling to these, without realizing that chasing after them cannot lead to either freedom or awakening.

Nonetheless, in her very life, in everything she did, she was an example of the true freedom and wisdom that arise from this very basic, fundamental essence that we all have – that we are. She showed that because we are all interconnected, we can deeply understand what's going on with others, and that the intentions we give rise to can manifest and function in the world.

All of these are in a sense side effects, things that arise naturally when we are truly one with everyone and everything around us. They happen because we are able to flow in harmony with our world, with no dualistic views or attachments to get in the way. At this point, other beings are not cut off from us; they are another aspect of ourselves. Who, feeling this to their very bones, could turn their back on others?

It was this deep compassion that made her a legend in Korea long before she formally started teaching. She was known for having the spiritual power to help people in all circumstances and with every kind of problem. She compared compassion to freeing a fish from a drying puddle, putting a homeless family into a home, or providing the school fees that would allow a student to finish high school. And when she did things like this, and more, few knew that she was behind it.

Her compassion was also unconditional. She would offer what help she could to individuals and organizations, whether they be Christian or Buddhist, a private organization or governmental. She would help nun's temples that had no relationship with her temple, Christian organizations that looked after children living on their own, city-run projects to help care for the elderly, and much, much more. Yet, even when she provided material support, always there was the deep, unseen aid she offered through this connection we all share.

However, she also saw that ultimately, for people to live freely and go forward in the world as a blessing to all around them, they needed to know about this bright essence that is within each of us. To help people discover this for themselves, she founded the first *Hanmaum*[5] Seon Center in 1972.

---

5. Hanmaum [han-ma-um]: Han means one, great, and combined, while maum means mind, as well as heart, and together they mean everything combined and connected as one.

What is called Hanmaum is intangible, unseen, and transcends time and space. It has no beginning or end, and is sometimes called our fundamental mind. It also means the mind of all beings and everything in the universe connected and working together as one. In English, we usually translate this as one mind.

For the next forty years she gave wisdom to those who needed wisdom, food and money to those who were poor and hungry, and compassion to those who were hurting.

Daehaeng Kun Sunim founded ten overseas branches of Hanmaum Seon Center, and her teachings have been translated into twelve different languages to date: English, German, Russian, Chinese, French, Spanish, Indonesian, Italian, Japanese, Vietnamese, Estonian, and Czech, in addition to the original Korean. For more information about these or the overseas centers, please see the back of this book.

Dharma Talk 1

Dancing on the Whirlwind

June 16, 1996

This talk was first published in English
as Volume 17 in the ongoing series,
Practice in Daily Life.

Thank you so much for gathering together like this in spite of the bad weather and crowded space.

As I mentioned last time, this daily life of ours is like walking on a frozen lake, all the while trying to juggle a hundred different things. And the ice is thin. Very thin.

Would you stop and build a campfire on such ice? No. But that's what happens when we get angry.

People don't realize just how thin the ice is, yet they build a fire there and keep feeding it with anger, blame, resentment, and attempts to dominate and control others. How soon before the ice gives way? How long before they're left flailing and struggling, trying to escape the freezing water? They certainly won't be taking any more steps forward on their own path.

Suppose this building was on fire. Finding a way out would be the only thing on your mind. Every other problem would be forgotten. Learning how to rely upon your *fundamental mind*[6] and free yourself is exactly this urgent.

It's the only thing I've ever paid attention to. Ever since I was little, all my focus was on going forward while entrusting everything to this fundamental mind, and learning how to be free from the bonds of this *middle realm*.[7] Health, money, eating well, living comfortably – these aren't unimportant, but I have no interest in them. What truly matters is helping people understand how they can free themselves.

---

6. Fundamental mind: This refers to our inherent essence, that which we fundamentally are. "Mind," in Mahayana Buddhism, almost never means the brain or intellect. Instead it refers to this essence, through which we are inherently connected to everything, everywhere. It is intangible, beyond space and time, and has no beginning or end. It is the source of everything, and everyone is endowed with it. "Fundamental Mind" is interchangeable with other terms such as "Buddha-nature," "True nature," "True self," and "Foundation."

7. Middle realm(world)**:** In Buddhism, the realm of human beings is sometimes described as the "middle realm" or "the middle world," because it is said to be one of six realms. It exists below the realms of more advanced beings, called devas and asuras, but above the realms of animals, hungry ghosts, and the various hell states.

This is all I've paid attention to and all I'll ever do. Learning how to free yourself is the most urgent thing any of us can do.

Sakyamuni *Buddha*[8] showed us how we should live when he said, *"Form*[9] is *emptiness,*[10] and emptiness is form. Thus, everything is already flowing naturally and freely."* However, people don't fully realize the implications of this.

---

8. Buddha: In this text, "Buddha" is capitalized out of respect, because these represent the essence and function of the enlightened mind. "The Buddha" always refers to Sakyamuni Buddha.

9. Form: In Korean, the Sino-Korean character for form (色) also includes things like emotions, evaluations, and views. It can be described as the material world and the experiences, emotions, and thoughts arising from the interactions taking place within it.

10. Emptiness: Emptiness is not a void, but rather refers to the ceaseless flowing of all things. Everything is flowing as part of one whole, so there is nothing that can be separated out and set aside as if it existed independently of everything else. There is, therefore, no "me" that exists apart from other people or other things. There is only the interpenetrated and interdependent whole, "empty" of any independent or separate selves or objects.

Sakyamuni Buddha was telling us that our mind is utterly limitless, unhindered by anything, and unfathomably mysterious. This mind of ours is utterly free of all fixed forms, so if we use our minds wisely, we can be free from the limitations of this sack of flesh. We can be free from this bubble of air we're trapped in, this middle realm.[11]

Everything is Flowing, So What's There to Carry with You?

Sometimes I say, "There is no such thing as karma," or "There is no suffering." However, we experience both of these, don't we? So why do I say they don't exist? Because everything keeps flowing without ceasing.

When you're at home, sometimes you're a father, sometimes you become a husband, and then when you go to work, you're someone else. Everything you experience in life is ceaselessly changing like this – what you see, what you hear, what you say,

---

11. "Bubble of air" and "middle realm" refer to the Earth and the material world as we normally perceive it.

where you go – all of it just flies by. Even the words "flies by" can't adequately describe this. Yet I have to use some kind of words to convey a sense of this.

When you came up to the *Dharma*[12] Hall today, you just walked up, taking one step after another, right? You didn't try to cling to each footstep, did you? Each time you lifted your foot, that previous footstep disappeared as if it had never happened. It's there and gone in an instant, with nothing in it to cling to.

Everything you see, hear, and experience is like this. It's all just brushing past us, flowing naturally. From the very beginning it's flowed like this, without cease. Think about what this means for your life.

People actually do have different levels of spirituality. There are some people who are very deep, others who are quite shallow, and the rest are somewhere in between. Even here today, some people can easily follow me, while others have a hard time. But these levels aren't fixed things; they

---

12. Dharma: This refers to both ultimate truth, and the truth taught by the Buddha.

aren't permanent states. If you want to raise your level, then listen carefully to what I'm going to say and try to apply it. Work hard at it and jump!

Please listen carefully: Not a single thing is fixed and unchanging. Nothing you see, hear, or do remains the same. The moment you meet someone, the instant you arrive somewhere, it all flows away and is gone. There's nothing to grab hold of, so what is there that you would claim as something "I did"?

Both the "I" of that moment, as well as all the things "I did," are already gone. All the things that "I saw," as well as the "me" who saw them, have vanished. The "me" who was there listening, as well as everything "I heard" are gone. There's no instant in which karma or suffering could stick to you. Even here, it's not an issue of there being some place for these things to stick to, it's that there's no instant for any of that to happen. There's no moment for karma, suffering, or happiness to stick to anything. Let alone any place where they could stick.

You and everything you see flies by in an instant. You, the person who's hearing, as well as what you hear, what you do, what you feel, the people you encounter – all are there and gone. And there's certainly no instant when something could be stuck to something else.

Nonetheless, people see something and then talk and talk about it. They hear something, and talk and talk about it. At the drop of a hat, they give rise to so many opinions and judgments. It all wants to flow, but they won't let it. I'm not saying that it's bad to talk and think about things, but you also need to be aware that everything is flowing and circulating as one, naturally. So when you speak, do it while letting go of any traces of "I," as well as any judgments or discriminations.

When you're truly aware of how everything is flowing and working together as one whole, then whatever you do will naturally be free of any trace of discrimination or distinction between "you" and "others." Thus, the things you do and say won't end up creating more karma or suffering. So love others, but do it unconditionally. Listen to others, but do it while letting go of any traces of "I." Learn and study, but do it while letting go of any thoughts of "I know."

The reason I'm telling you this is that if you understand how everything works together as one through this fundamental mind of ours, and go forward trying to apply this truth to your daily life, then even though you continue to live in this world, you'll be able to function far above the human realm. In other words, while taking care of all your ordinary responsibilities in this material realm, you can also work through the unseen realm to help with problems, both seen and unseen, around the world.

If you work diligently at trying to apply this fundamental mind to your daily life, then you will be able to guide all of the *karmic consciousnesses*[13]

---

13. Karmic consciousnesses(業識)**:** Our thoughts, feelings, and behaviors are recorded as the consciousnesses of the lives that make up our body. These are sometimes called karmic consciousnesses, although they don't have independent awareness or volition. Sometime afterwards, these consciousnesses will come back out.

Thus we may feel happy, sad, angry, etc., without an obvious reason, or they may cause other problems to occur. The way to dissolve these consciousnesses is not to react to them when they arise, and instead to entrust them to our foundation. However, even these consciousnesses are just temporary combinations, so we shouldn't cling to the concept of them.

within you, as well as those beings you've created *karmic affinity*[14] with as you've passed through life after life. And you'll be able to do this while being present in the world, taking care of your body, and taking care of the people and things that are part of your ordinary, daily life. You will ignore none of these, yet they will have no more pull on you than your dirty laundry. Freely, easily, you'll let go of everything, and thus obtain everything. As you obtain everything, you will be able to give it all to others. Work hard and make this happen!

Hold onto Your Center and Let Everything Flow

People tend to make all kinds of judgments based on what they see or hear, but you really shouldn't tie yourself up in fixed views like this. When Sakyamuni Buddha wanted to save an insect, sometimes he became that insect. He had to first become one with that creature's mind, and then it wouldn't resist his help.

---

14. Karmic affinity (因縁): The connection or attraction between people or things, due to previous karmic relationships.

Years ago, when I was walking through a forest, I came across a crawfish sitting in the middle of the trail. It had ended up quite a ways from the nearby stream, so I bent down, intending to pick it up and carry it back to the water. But as I reached for the crawfish, it held up its claws, waving them at me as if to fight me off. As soon as I saw this, I knew what the Buddha had meant: In order to save a crawfish, you have to become one with it. Even a crawfish!

Although we ourselves now have a human shape, we're filled with consciousnesses of every kind of level. These unenlightened consciousnesses give rise to every kind of feeling and thought. Sometimes they make us happy, at other times they cause us to feel miserable, and at still other times they cause us to feel angry.

But they're deceiving us. Those thoughts are arising from inside us, so we mistake them for "me," thinking they are "my" feelings. We act on them and make choices based on them. And this is how life becomes suffering.

Yet it's said, "There is no suffering." This is because every single thing you do and experience keeps transforming every instant. It's all flowing like water, like clouds gathering and then drifting away. But here we are, insisting things should be like this, or people should be doing that. As if we had control over any of it! As if we could catch the clouds or grab water in our fists!

How could trying to grab hold of such things lead anywhere other than to suffering? If you're wise enough to just let these things flow past, you can avoid so much unnecessary suffering.

There's not a single thing anywhere that's fixed or stationary. All of it is ceaselessly changing and transforming and flowing away. Thus, it's called empty. Even "I" doesn't exist. Within your body, "I" is a collection of cells and lives that are ceaselessly flowing and changing. Outside your body, this "I" is also part of a ceaselessly changing whole. Each aspect is flowing and transforming, with nothing stationary that we can separate out and label. It's all empty.

Thus, there is no stationary place for illness to stick to, nor any place for suffering to stick to. There's no place for karma, no place for sadness, and no place for even joy to remain.

Think about going to see a movie: It plays for a couple of hours, and then it's over and the curtain comes down. And then, before long, the next movie starts. Our lives, too, are like this. So regardless of what kind of role you're playing, go forward holding fast to your own upright center. All you truly need to do is just hold onto this.

Like a wheel rotates around its axle, we have to make our fundamental mind the center of our lives. We have to live with this great *pillar of mind*[15] at our center. No matter what happens, this pillar never wavers. It's capable of sending forth vast, unimaginable energy. So have faith in this center of yours, rely upon it, and entrust everything there. Unconditionally! Unleash this energy and go forward applying it to everything in your life.

---

15. Pillar of mind: Similar to Jujangja (拄杖子), which is a monk's staff, but the term is used figuratively to refer to our fundamental mind.

Even when things are going well, even when they go badly, even if your role in life seems meaningless, or even if it seems important – regardless of whether you're male or female, sophisticated or clumsy, rich or poor, young or old – when you go forward centered around this great pillar of mind, your life will flow like water. A wheel that's centered on its axle won't come off.

This pillar of mind can be called Buddha-nature, "my true abode," or "the saving power of *Prajna*."[16] It can be given all kinds of names, but regardless of the label, if you rely upon that place, if you utterly entrust everything there, to the extent that you are able to work together as one with everything, without any trace of "me," then you will be able to live in every moment naturally, attuned to the flowing of the whole. Just as you are, you can lead a life of great meaning and worth.

---

16. Prajna: Insight into the true nature of reality, namely the awareness of impermanence, emptiness, and non-self.

Looking around, it seems like some of you are still unclear about what I'm saying. Yet, as the saying goes, once you understand one thing, ten others will become clear. Everything in your daily life is already flowing away, so what's there to be unclear about? It's all changing and transforming every instant.

Look at what's happening in your life – it's all teaching you. "Ah, everything is flowing like water. This is how I need to live as well!" Go forward like this without trying to grasp or cling to things. If you try to seize hold of something, it will become a source of suffering.

Not only is there no moment in your life that you could grab hold of something, there's also no moment for anyone else to grab hold of something. Even the Buddha can't awaken you or raise your spiritual level. He can't bring you happiness, nor can he take it away from you. Everything comes or goes according to our own thoughts and actions. It comes and goes according to the decisions we've made.

Everything is flowing by so quickly that there's no moment of time that you could grab and say, "That's what I've done," or "I didn't do that." It's all flowing and changing every instant in response to what you are doing and thinking.

This Treasure Can Take Care of Everything

You need to know this: Whatever hardship you're facing, whatever illness or suffering you're going through, ultimately those all have only one cause – your own mind. It's the *habits*,[17] desires, and attachments you've created through life after life. Don't try to figure out your past life, and don't worry about your future. Even this very moment is empty. Everything passes by. Everything is going away at every instant. Yet, even though I tell people this, they still try to cling to things.

I'm not saying to never have opinions or speak, just that when you do, you need to let go of your

---

17. Habits (習)**:** These include not just the ways of thought and behavior learned in this life, but also all of those tendencies of thought and behavior that have accumulated over endless eons.

Dancing on the Whirlwind 35

attachments and grasping to whatever it is. Also when you're working on something, pay attention to how things are flowing. Keep entrusting everything like this. Then you'll be able to respond to the situation naturally and harmoniously. "Last year we handled that problem like this. Would that work now?" Being able to respond from your foundation like this is so important.

Everything in your life depends upon where your thoughts, words, and actions are coming from.

When I say that you need to cling to this pillar of mind, I mean that you need to entrust everything there, utterly and unconditionally, without looking back. But people often miss this point, and instead just keep repeating the words "pillar of mind" or "*Juingong*."[18] Merely repeating the names like this

---

18. Juingong (主人空): Pronounced "ju-in-gong." Juin (主人) means the true doer or the master, and gong (空) means empty. Thus Juingong is our true nature, our true essence, the master within, which is always changing and manifesting, without a fixed form or shape.

Daehaeng Sunim has compared Juingong to the root of the tree. Our bodies and consciousness are like the branches and leaves, but it is the root that is the source of the tree, and it is the invisible root beneath the ground that sustains the visible tree.

is just reaching deep into your own suffering and grasping it that much tighter.

In fact, even the foundation, Juingong, that we rely upon is just a name, a word. So we have to entrust everything without holding onto even that.

Although I keep saying, "You need to entrust this pillar of mind with everything and then just let all things in your daily life flow in tune with it," there are still some people who are just repeating the words "Juingong" and "pillar of mind." As if that would do any good.

If you keep working on utterly relying upon and trusting your own pillar of mind, your Juingong, and are entrusting it with every thought, every worry, every problem that arises, you will find gratitude and joy in the middle of all that. And when you are sad, you will find solace and a shoulder to cry upon. This fundamental mind of yours is a treasure that can take care of everything. It's such a treasure!

A Single Thought is So Precious!

So make a very firm decision that "This fundamental mind is the only thing I'm going to rely upon!" If you entrust everything with this attitude, it will all naturally flow towards the best outcome. However, if your desire for something is greater than your willingness to let go, you'll end up assessing things through the eyes of covetousness, foolishness, and desperation. And then you'll start meddling and getting wrapped up in all kinds of things. Do you know how much noise some people make when they see dried dog poop on the sidewalk? It's just old dog poop! [Laughs.]

When I scatter birdseed in the yard, the birds all go to the seed that's farthest away from people. They go where there's no people moving around. If you want them to enjoy that birdseed, you have to step back and leave them alone.

People need to work at relying upon their foundation, but instead they spend their time blaming others or complaining about what they're doing, or even meddling in their lives. Do you really have time for that? The house is on fire! You have only a few moments to find a way out! Are you really going to spend this time standing around criticizing others?

In the case of parents and children, there's already a close connection there, so if you just rely upon your pillar of mind and trust it, things between you will work out quite well. But careless words will make a mess of your relationship. Instead of trying to actually get in touch with their own fundamental mind, some people shout at their children, saying things like, "What the hell are you doing? Why aren't you doing your homework? Do you think you're so smart that you don't even need to study for exams?"

If your home is filled with arguing and shouting over every little thing, if, when your children complain about how hard school is or about problems with other kids, they hear in return, "You don't know what hard is! My life is hard! Do you know how hard I work to…," they won't thrive. If they don't feel any warmth at home, if it isn't a comfortable place, they'll stay away as much as possible, or even run away.

So you must let go of everything and just rely upon this one pillar of mind. In truth, everything is already flowing, so just try to not cling to ideas or events. If, with a wise thought, you can leap over these things, your life and family will be relaxed and comfortable. Wouldn't this be a better way to live?

What I've just said is the most important thing I'll say all day. It's so precious! Our lives continuously flow and change, as fast and ceaselessly as a spinning propeller. In the midst of all this flowing, there's no place for anything to stick to.

Even though I tell people that there's inherently no place for illness to stick to, they don't seem to believe it. I'm just telling you about how the world works, nothing more, and yet people still don't make an effort to live in accordance with this. Instead, they follow distorted paths, living upside-down lives, and end up experiencing every kind of hardship.

If they could just live in tune with this truth that everything is already flowing and moving through their fundamental mind, they would radiate joy and wisdom, and would live out their full, proper span of years.

Learn the Ways of a Free Person

Let me be clear, what you attain through this practice won't fade away. It will be with you forever. Why? Because it's something you'll use continuously as you evolve.

Ultimately, if you keep working at this, you will be free. Free to choose your shape, free to choose the level you'll be reborn at, free to be born on this planet or to choose another planet, or even a star, or somewhere else entirely. You'll be able to choose whatever kind of life you want to have going forward.

Even though everyone is inherently free, you have to learn how to behave freely in order to actually become free. You need to learn to take what you understand, put it into practice, and keep doing this. Start with where you are. Look at how we build a house. You start by leveling the dirt and building a solid foundation. Then you need to build the walls, floor, and roof. You have to figure out how to do all of this to end up with a useful building.

Even to build just a house, there are so many things you have to know and be able to do. How much more is there, then, if you want to know what it truly means to be free? So you'd better get started learning these things one by one, and stage by stage.

This is why the Buddha tested his disciples, asking, "Have you grasped my skin?" "Have you grasped my flesh?" "Have you grasped my bones?" and, "Have you grasped my essence?" *Seon*[19] masters have said similar things to their students.

---

19. Seon (禪) (Chan, Zen)**:** Seon describes the unshakeable state where one has firm faith in their inherent foundation, their Buddha-nature, and so returns everything they encounter back to this fundamental mind. It also means letting go of "I," "me," and "mine" throughout one's daily life.

That said, you shouldn't concern yourself with other people's level of spiritual practice, or compare yourself to them. Just focus on putting into practice what you've learned, and then move on from that. If you keep doing this over and over, you'll naturally begin to understand everything about different levels of spiritual awareness.

Sometimes when people come to me with some desperate problem, I'll tell them very specifically what to do, and that will usually take care of it. So, they've gotten past one particularly ugly problem, but when the next thing arises, what will happen to them? Will their only hope be to go find someone else to take care of it for them? Will this be their life every time something ugly arises? If that's the case, it won't turn out well.

This is why I keep urging you to work at relying upon your fundamental mind and to learn how it works. That said, the deeper your practice goes, the more you'll realize there is no "I know" or "I gained," because you'll understand that everything is constantly flowing as one, and that not a single thing has been added. You have to truly and sincerely put this into practice, and then you can take care of whatever arises. If you can see whatever confronts you as part of yourself, as something that's not separate, then even if all the ghosts in the world were to swarm at you, you'd just smile and chuckle.

Why? Because you're one with them. The fingers on one hand never hurt each other, do they? It's the same reality.

When it comes to people suffering from severe mental illness, well, often they can't practice for themselves, so the family has to work that much harder at practicing so that they can connect with them through their fundamental mind. In this way, family can bring the energy of our fundamental mind to bear on the situation. Of course, I also do what I can to help by giving them some of the energy of my mind, or, if they've lived a gentle, generous life, I can put their mind into mine.

If someone persistently works at having faith in their inherent Buddha-nature, and is trying to trust it with whatever comes up, they too can be a light to those who suffer.

In cases of mental illnesses like this, no amount of pills or therapy will completely cure the illness. There are some things that doctors can help with, but they can't solve problems caused by the consciousnesses of the lives within us. These consciousnesses were created and conditioned through interactions with karma, genetics, ghosts, microbes, and the conditioned nature of existence, and so the only real way to dissolve them is through our fundamental mind.

Thus, the best way to help people in this situation is to help them through mind so that they can eventually take all of these karmic consciousnesses and return them to their own fundamental mind.

Remind them that everything is working together as one in this flowing whole, and encourage them to put their mind at ease and quickly move through the things that confront them, entrusting them one by one, and then moving on.

If you, too, go forward like this, focused on only your fundamental mind, this great pillar, then no matter how bitter a wind should blow, you won't be swept off your feet. In a word, take it all and introduce it to your fundamental mind. In this way, you'll be able to help the patients as well as their families get through the illness.

If the mind has problems, then it's through this fundamental mind that those must be solved. In fact, every last thing in the world is something that's been created through mind. Your mind is what caused you to be born into this world, it created the life you lead now, so it's what can take care of all this and help you fulfill the role you were born to play. Understand that no one else assigned you this role. You made it and assigned it to yourself.

But please understand that even this role is just a temporary thing. None of it is anything to get attached to. If you aren't reaching out and trying to grab onto karma, then karma, too, has no way to stick to you. Hardships won't find a place to grab hold, and illnesses, likewise, won't be able to find a foothold.

Keep this wonderful fact in mind and stay focused on Juingong. Stay focused on your foundation like it was a lifeline, and entrust everything there with gratitude. Develop your ability to cope with whatever comes to you by taking everything, in each moment, and entrusting it to your fundamental mind.

Then, whatever adversity you face will change. If you go forward with nothing more in life than this ability, it will still be enough for you to live without undue want or hardship.

Stop Digging the Hole, and Instead Trust Your Inherent Light

It's completely understandable if you don't yet grasp what I'm saying. But the reason I keep saying you need to trust your foundation and entrust everything to it is because that is the only way you can develop the deep ability to truly solve whatever you face. This is the only way to truly live peacefully and at ease, regardless of what arises in your life. If you can do this, you've taken one giant step forward on the path.

But instead, people get caught up in thoughts like "How could I practice like *Kun Sunim*[20] does? I don't know what I'm doing! I'm not at the same level she is." It's these thoughts that are the problem. People take situations and problems that they should have been able to pass through fairly quickly, and instead turn them into quagmires. They create all kinds of unnecessary work and hardship.

Then, after they've made things worse, they come to me, asking for help. It's so frustrating. I wish I could say how I really feel when they bring me these things! "Oh, for crying out loud! Why did you make such a mess out of something that wouldn't have caused any problems? Why do you keep blowing things up, and then asking me for help with them?"

---

20. Sunim / Kun Sunim: Sunim is the respectful title of address for a Buddhist monk or nun in Korea, and Kun Sunim is the title given to outstanding nuns or monks.

But I can't say these things out loud! Instead, I just look for what people need to move forward and go from there. "Okay. Focus on entrusting it all and observing. If you're sincerely letting go, then my mind will be there as well, and will help you. So deeply, truly, trust your root and turn everything over to it. Then, just go forward while being aware."

Before long, they come back, saying, "It worked! Thank you so much!" But frankly, sometimes this leaves me feeling frustrated and irritated, because they keep making an unnecessary mess out of things time after time, so that it doesn't seem like they've learned anything at all.

So sometimes I'll respond with, "'Thanks?' Thanks for what? It turned out well because you worked at trusting your own fundamental mind. You have your own fundamental mind, as do I. These are like electrical wires, and when they connect, the energy flows back and forth, and the light comes on. If you want to thank something, then feel grateful to this fundamental mind, this Juingong of yours that made that possible." I truly didn't appreciate just how hard it is to get people to have faith in this treasure they're carrying around within themselves.

Even if it takes every last drop of my blood, I want to make everyone grasp just one thing: Deeply trust this foundation of yours, and entrust every single thing there. Let go and entrust it. Only then will you be free in the truest sense, and able to move beyond the limitations of the human realm.

This is the way you can save yourself, and the way you can save the world. I want nothing more than for you all to awaken to this truth. This is the focus of all my efforts. Even if someone were to offer me all the kingdoms of the Earth, I wouldn't turn away from this.

Even if someone brings a van full of cash and asks me to solve some problem they're facing, it's pointless if they don't have faith in their foundation. If they don't trust their own foundation, there's no energy going back and forth, and so no benefit can come from their offering.

I didn't become a sunim for the sake of living off your offerings. If I did, I'd deserve death. Actually, setting aside the issue of dying, living like that would lower the level of my existence so much that in my next life I would naturally be drawn towards the body of a burrowing insect.

But if it's necessary to help you, I'm not afraid of being born with even that shape. But don't worry, I know how to escape from that! [Sunim and the audience laugh.]

It looks like there are people who want to ask questions today, so let me say just one more thing: When we walk, we just go forward naturally, don't we? Is there anyone who stops and tries to cling to each footprint? No. So in the rest of your daily life as well, go forward freely, letting go of everything. Then, because everything is inherently flowing and changing without cease, there will be no place for illness to stick to, no place for karma to land, and no place for hardships to grab hold of you.

Because everything is flowing like this, the thoughts you give rise to have a huge influence.

They can cause your family to thrive, or to fall into a dark place from which it may never arise. It's unfortunate that even though I tell people about this in such detail, so many of them still don't seem to be able to put it into practice. They go and put themselves in desperate situations, where they face losing everything, even their home.

Then, because the situation is so desperate, and they're suffering so much, I have no choice but to give them something miraculous to hang onto. I have no choice because the situation is so bad and they don't yet have the skills to get themselves out of it. So I may tell them that if they work sincerely and truly at entrusting their situation, then someone special will appear and help them. I hope you understand how much I hate having to say things like this in order to get people to start trusting their foundation. Anyway, then, through this inner Buddha, I arrange for help to find them.

Listen, when you hurt, I hurt too. When you cry a bucket full of tears, I shed two or three. It's that painful. When I help people, sometimes I have to become a maggot or a tick. But I'm not afraid of that because I know that even those forms aren't fixed and unchanging.

Please think carefully about the implications of this, and don't be afraid of letting go and trusting your foundation, no matter what arises. Don't let anything intimidate you! Even if you are about to die, don't be afraid. Even if the world is about to explode, don't be afraid. Even if your job and savings disappear, don't be afraid. If you rely upon your own centered mind, standing up straight and without fear, then the unseen energy all around you will take notice and will respond to your centered mind, helping you find a way forward.

There are all kinds of stories about this kind of help. Stories about the Bodhisattva of Compassion, or the Hermit Sage, or Dharma-Protecting Warriors. Here in Korea, we even have them in children's cartoons. You've all seen the one with Master Cabbage and Master Radish,[21] haven't you? They

---

21. These were two superhero-type characters from the Korean cartoon series, "Once Upon a Time" (옛날 옛적에).

transform their bodies into any thing or life that's needed, and then go help people. This is the functioning of a *bodhisattva*.[22]

So there's no reason to be scared. You all have this kind of a bodhisattva within you. Right there, within you, are Buddhas, bodhisattvas, and Dharma protectors. So what's there to be scared of? There's no limit to the number of helpers you have within you. Even if you have a million of them within you, they fit perfectly, without any crowding. And even if you use a million of them, they never decrease. Now, if you still don't understand, I'm not sure what else I can say! [Laughs.]

---

22. Bodhisattva (菩薩)**:** This usually refers to a person of great spiritual ability who is dedicated to saving those lost in ignorance and suffering. But it also means the applied energy of our fundamental nature, used to help save beings. It can also be described as the non-dual wisdom of enlightenment being used to help others awaken for themselves.

Be Humble
Even When You Have Money and Power

Questioner 1 (Male) I've noticed that during those times when my life is going well, I don't think much about spiritual practice. When times were hard, I'd often thought about the things I could do for others if I had some real money, but then when I had money, I mostly used it for myself.

It seems that if my life is comfortable, I forget about spiritual practice. It feels like I also lose my compassion for others. It seems as if people don't take an interest in spiritual practice until they're faced with adversity and desperate circumstances. Could you please speak about this?

Kun Sunim I've said something similar before, that it often takes adversity to get people working at spiritual practice. While this is true in general, it doesn't have to be this way. What it truly depends upon is how you make up your mind. If you're in a good situation, you can still practice without a lot of hardship or suffering. There's no need to create a bunch of pain in order to practice.

That said, you realize that money and property aren't yours, right? Understand that those things are only something you're managing on behalf of the whole, and live humbly and frugally. Understand that you're going through all of this because you are still only functioning at the human level of development. You're still only at the human level, so be humble in how you respond to the things you face. Don't forget to care for the land that has raised you. Don't forget how much your grandparents and parents suffered for the sake of their children.

Knowing all this, live humbly, as the manager of what comes your way. There's a lot of wisdom in the old expressions, "The ripest grain bows low" and "The branches with the most fruit hang the lowest." While there are people who live extravagantly and recklessly, those working at spiritual practice should try to live modestly, whether they have money or not.

Donating money to help build a temple isn't the only way to support Buddhism. Helping people in need is also doing the Buddha's work.[23] There are families where the parents are sick, and the children miss meals. There are elderly people with no children to look after them, and orphaned adolescents who are trying to care for their younger brothers and sisters. Some of these people are lucky enough to come to the attention of TV news programs, and so receive a fair amount of help, but there are many, many more no one ever hears about. Some people are too ashamed to tell their story to others, and some have so much pride they insist on doing everything by themselves, but all of them are struggling each day just to live. There are so many people living like this, hidden from sight.

---

23. In Korean, the term used here, bul-sa (佛事), has taken on a sense of supporting the construction of temple buildings. Being quite expensive, these require a lot of support and time to finish. But here Daehaeng Sunim is reminding readers of its original meaning, which is closer to "the work of a Buddha."

So, what I'm saying is that there is no shortage of people in need of your help. Just be sure to do it as spiritual practice, while letting go of any thoughts of "I did." Even if you have no money at all, there is still that portion of helping that you can do through mind.

No matter how much you use this fundamental mind of yours, its energy never decreases. Would you just put it away in a closet and never use it? Give everyone who comes a full helping! Don't be stingy. Don't discriminate between the people you like and those you can't stand. People who use their minds like that won't be able to awaken, nor will they be able to master the use of their fundamental mind.

How to Embrace Others

Questioner 2 (Male) For a long time, I've had a sense that when we are born into this world, each one of us brings a blank sheet of paper. It's completely empty, and we can write anything we want to, and use it in any way we want. Some people write stories, others draw pictures, still others filter alcohol through it, and some people even dump their trash on it.

Of course, this paper is infinite, never stained, and can't be damaged. Yet when I see people use it recklessly, I check my own behavior, thinking, "I need to use my mind wisely. I have to get my act together. I need to go forward in the right direction." And I remind myself that everything I'm encountering is part of the process of learning and evolving. I understand that spiritual practice is necessary for my own well-being, but we also need to use it for the well-being of others because this truth of *one mind* [24] is the truth that we are all living and working together.

---

24. One mind (한마음 [han-ma-um]): From the Korean, where "one" has a nuance of great and combined, while "mind" is more than intellect and includes "heart" as well. Together, they mean everything combined and connected as one. What is called "one mind" is intangible, unseen, and transcends time and space. It has no beginning or end, and is sometimes called our fundamental mind. It also means the mind of all beings and everything in the universe connected and working together as one.

So my problem is this: I can let go when it's something that benefits me, but when it's necessary for others, I have a really hard time. Can you give me some advice about how I can overcome this?

Kun Sunim This fundamental mind of ours! It functions completely, with no distinction between inside or outside. It's utterly empty and serene. Actually, we can't even use words like "serene" because all words and descriptions fail to even scratch its essence.

This fundamental mind encompasses everything, without the least discrimination, so if you're thinking about practice in terms of "for myself" or "for others," then you've gone astray. When something confronts you, and you raise and entrust an intention for that, do so while letting go of any distinctions of "you" versus "me."

If you go forward like this, letting go of both sides, things will naturally work out well for you and for others, and make it possible for everyone involved to live together non-dually.

Nonetheless, you still need to pay attention to doing things wisely. For example, even though you sincerely want to help someone, if your words are likely to upset or irritate them, then don't say anything at all. Instead, work through this fundamental mind, raising generous, harmonious intentions, and then entrust those to your foundation.

If you're talking with them and it looks like they're open to what you'd say, then that's fine. But even in that case, it's better to be a bit indirect and just nudge them. There may be lots of books about Buddhism these days, but it's only when we can put our knowledge into practice like this that our lives will begin to improve. All of our lives. All together, as one whole.

Freeing Yourself from Resentment

Questioner 3 (Male) Hello, I've noticed that when things at work don't go well, I find myself really resenting the people responsible. Likewise, if someone harasses me or deliberately causes me problems, I end up wishing that something bad would happen to them. However, when I come here and listen to your Dharma talks, I realize that I shouldn't be thinking like that. Yet when Monday comes around, it starts all over again. Can you make these thoughts disappear, or at least cause them to not arise so often?

Kun Sunim [Laughs.] No one else can do that for you. The person who can take care of that is the one you see in the mirror every day. That's who moves your body and makes things happen. Your car doesn't drive itself, right? It's the driver who checks the oil and gas, and works at avoiding accidents.

Just like this, it's your foundation, your Juingong, that moves and directs you. So entrust everything there. Even if someone approaches you with evil intent, completely entrust that to your foundation, thinking, "Inherently his mind and my mind are connected. The foundation of all life is one, and this mind that exists before any thoughts arose is also one. So, true self, Juingong, brighten this light within him and make our minds one again." Know that your foundation is taking care of this, and completely entrust everything.

Let go of hatred and resentment. Just entrust all of that to your foundation and live peacefully. The fact is, your opinions, judgments, and perceptions keep you from seeing the whole. They prevent you from understanding what's really going on. So don't get caught up in thoughts like "He ruined my life." As you work at your ordinary, daily life, when you have some conflicts or problems with people, don't worry or obsess over those. That's useless. Just entrust all of it to your foundation. Even if it seems like someone is trying to harm or slander you, entrust that as well.

Even though they had bad intent, that situation could turn into something good for you in the end. Or it may be the case that you misunderstood their actions entirely.

So don't get caught up in your opinions and judgments, nor in replaying the situation over and over. Just entrust the whole thing to your foundation, knowing, "Juingong! Let's all live together harmoniously, and allow the inner light we all have to become brighter." Know that your foundation is what can make all of this happen. Then, the other person's mind will become brighter, and your relationships can become more harmonious. And if one of you did something wrong, you may become aware of it and apologize. This is how you can become warmer towards each other.

Giving Back and How to Finish Things Up Well

Questioner 4 (Male) I'd like to ask you about the idea of "giving back" when we've finished something.[25]

---

25. Literally, "returning back" (回向). In Korean Buddhism, this implies the practice of giving back or sharing with others at the successful conclusion of something. While it's understood that this is a good thing to do, and will also benefit oneself and one's ancestors, it doesn't have the strong nuance of "transferring merit to one's ancestors" that it has in Chinese Buddhism.

When something finishes or some problem works itself out, we often try to give something back to others, knowing that's an important part of finishing things well. People often sense that what we share with others ends up helping us.

Although hardships and difficulties can cause us to grow, no one actually wants them. In fact, it seems that for a lot of people, when they say they're entrusting those problems, they're really just trying to wish them away.

Anyway, although we try to give back at the end of something, what about the case where suffering never seems to finish? People often seem to lose their hope and focus when hardships go on and on.

It seems to me that it's better to view and accept the hardships we face as something that has come to teach us. Even though those are not something we want, we still have to face them, so if we take them as a chance to learn, we can get through them a little easier. The act of viewing things positively like this feels like it becomes energy that feeds and sustains my practice.

That energy helps me face my suffering and overcome it, and will perhaps even lead me to awakening. So it seems to me that "giving back" isn't for the end, when something's finished, but rather, it's what we should do even while in the middle of our suffering. Am I understanding this correctly?

Kun Sunim You're not wrong, but people's lives are very different, so how they give back and how they view what confronts them are likewise very different. Although they think of all this in different ways, the important point is finishing things up well. If you can do this, that giving back will be taken care of as well.

For example, you could finish your life drinking every day and leave your family in chaos. You could cheat on your wife, leaving girlfriends and other children behind, with all of them at each other's throats. Or you could finish up leading a quiet, simple life. Or you could finish up while being deeply aware that you will end up reaping what you are sowing now.

But those people who are determined to awaken, work on returning every single thing every moment while they are alive. This isn't something you can do after you're dead.

Inherently, within this fundamental mind the past, present, and future function as one whole, so if, while alive, you return everything there, then those will melt down, and you'll be able to move beyond the chains of *samsara*[26] and its ceaseless cycle of rebirth and death.

This is why I'm always telling you that nirvana has to be attained while you're alive. It's not something that falls out of the sky after you're dead.

I'm talking about the kind of freedom that will allow you to manifest in any time or place, and endow you with the right and ability to hear, see, and act throughout the universe and *Dharma*

---

26. Samsara: The endless cycle of birth and death that all living things are continuously passing through.

realm.²⁷ This is what the Buddha meant when he said, "Dwelling in this vast sea of wisdom, you have received the *Ocean Seal*." ²⁸

When you're dead, nothing impinges upon you, either good or bad, so there's nothing to work with and no chance to hone your mind or spiritual ability. You have no chance to awaken to the great meaning, which was the whole purpose of being born as a human being in the first place.

Through this practice of knowing your fundamental mind, you can be free across all realms

---

27. Dharma realm (法界): The level of reality where everything functions as an interpenetrated and connected whole. Daehaeng Kun Sunim said that this can also be called the Dharma Net and compared it to our circulatory system, which connects and nourishes every single cell in the body.

28. Ocean Seal (海印): This term has a number of nuances, the most common of which is having, without a doubt (as if stamped with a seal), attained the state where the functioning of everything is perceived clearly and truly, like images seen on calm water. It also includes the nuance of horizons without end and depths that cannot be measured.

and states of living and dying, but you need a body to get to this point. There have to be things confronting you in order for you to develop wisdom. You have to be able to observe how your fundamental mind works with those obstacles. So this is why I'm always telling you that you have to attain nirvana while you're alive in order to shatter the chains of samsara.

Once you've transcended life and death, you realize that saying things like "the Buddha appeared," or, "the Buddha left," is just so much nonsense.

Thus, when you return absolutely everything to your foundation like this, you are truly "finishing things up well," and "giving back." This is why it's said that "giving back" is one of the paths to awakening.

To put it another way, if you take your children out, you should bring them home. Leaving the kids outside is not "finishing things up well," nor is it "giving back."

So don't tell people you'll take care of something that's beyond your ability. Know your own capacity. Work within your ability and leave things neatly wrapped up. This is how you give back.

People who tend to be reckless and irresponsible leave behind messes they can't take care of. They leave behind all kinds of loose ends. There's nothing about their lives that's wrapped up well. "Finishing things up well" and "giving back" are nothing other than taking good care of each thing as it arises in your life.

There's no need to be overwhelmed by this. If you live with the awareness that "I will reap what I sow," that's enough. This is easier than you think. There's no need for complicated oaths or vows – just view others as yourself. Think of their pain as your own pain. Try to know the limits of your own ability, have a realistic view of your place in the world, don't cause harm to others, and live together harmoniously.

For example, some people will lend money or sign loan guarantees out of a sense of loyalty or duty, but without reflecting upon their own circumstances. Although they meant well, they can end up causing horrible problems for their own family.

If you have enough money that you won't be bothered if a loan is never repaid, then go ahead and lend it if you want to. But when all you have is a house and a small plot of farmland, you have no business doing things that could cause your family to end up living under a bridge.

In no way whatsoever is lending money or signing a loan guarantee in these circumstances "giving back." Just being kind and good isn't what the Buddha taught. Not to mention the fact that signing those kinds of documents isn't actually a good or kind thing to do. There's neither wisdom nor kindness there. Leaving that sort of mess behind isn't what Sakyamuni Buddha taught. He taught us to be wise as well as kind. He showed how we can develop the wisdom and ability to truly benefit both others and ourselves. You've all heard of the *Buddha, Dharma, and Sangha*,[29] right?

Well, "Buddha" means the great, interconnected power and essential nature of our foundation. "Dharma" is a thought or intention arising from this, and "Sangha" is that thought and energy manifesting and functioning in the material world.

Think deeply about this and the implications it has for your own life, and live wisely, generously, and harmoniously.

---

29. Buddha, Dharma, and Sangha: Outwardly, these are Sakyamuni Buddha, his and other awakened beings' teachings about the truth, and the community of practitioners and the faithful. In this case Daehaeng Kun Sunim is explaining their inner aspects.

Dharma Talk 2

Turning Dirt into Gold

October 16, 1988

This talk was first published in English
as Volume 16 in the ongoing series,
Practice in Daily Life.

It's nice to see everyone here again. I'm sure that everyone here understands that we are always working together and interacting with each other. If you become aware of this fundamental mind of ours, and master how it really works, then you will also realize that all the great Seon masters of the past are always with you, and I too am always there with you. I don't remember exactly what I talked about last time, but I remember wishing that I had gone into more detail about this fundamental mind and how it works.

So, today, I'd like to talk about this in more depth. Let me start with the example of life and death. It is said that life and death cannot be separated from each other. But, as you probably already know, if you want to truly understand something, you must experience it for yourself. As it is, you are already experiencing things constantly arising and disappearing, aren't you?

Well, to use scientific terms, this fundamental mind of ours can be described as energy itself. The action of this mind manifesting itself, as it takes every kind of form according to the intentions we give rise to, can be compared to energy transforming into matter.

In the midst of all this, there is no separate life and death. Transforming and changing back and forth like this is what gets called "life and death." Many people think that living is one thing and dying another. But this isn't the case. Both are the interplay between matter and energy, all of which is possible because of our eternal root. It's also this eternal root, this eternal life, that makes it possible for us to flexibly give rise to every kind of intention.

Because our eternal root and the intentions we give rise to react together as one, we have a body, we can move and function, and we can interact with the people and the world around us. Our root is working with everything, and we are perfectly free to apply this principle to our lives and whatever confronts us.

Even though we have this unfathomable ability, if we don't learn to apply it, then when will we ever free ourselves from all the karma we've accumulated? How will we be able to step out of all the different hellish states of suffering? It's not only humans who suffer like this, but every other kind of life as well. Humans, animals, and insects have all created and brought with them unimaginable webs of karma.

What can we do, then, to be free from this karma? Go ahead and start with your body, for it is the collection of all your karma as well as innumerable chains of cause and effect. So start by taking 30 minutes or so in the evening, and try to reflect upon the fact that it was the functioning of all your karma and karmic connections that created your body. There's no need to go somewhere else to begin your spiritual practice. Everything you need to work with is right here! If you want to be truly free, this is the first thing you must remember.

Now, let me talk a bit about the essential points. As you've heard me say before, your body is composed of billions of unenlightened beings. Of course, each of these beings is a Buddha, but before awakening, we are all unenlightened beings. These unenlightened beings gather together according to their karmic affinity into one large collection of karma. They gather together and form this lump of flesh that gets called "me." It's this same principle of gathering together according to karmic affinity that has caused all of us to come together here today for this Dharma talk.

Let me give you an example of this karmic affinity. Suppose you treat someone badly because of what they did to you. Right or wrong, you've now created the causes that will bring you together in the future as well. If you beat an animal to death, that action and intention will create a certain kind of karmic attraction. Thus it happens that we are the lumps of flesh in which sufferings beyond number are gathered together. As we've tried to survive through the eons, is there any way to even guess at all of the terrible things we've done?

Don't think that this current life, what you're going through now, is all there is. You've already gone through endless lives before even making it to the human realm. Although, in truth, the distance between animals and human beings is no more than the thickness of a sheet of paper.

We've gone through life after life with untold different bodies, passing through light years of eons, so imagine all the karmic recordings we've created, and all of the series of causes and effects those have put into motion. Think about all the interactions and all the karmic affinities that must have been created over those eons. And now, although we have human shapes, these are due to all of those past affinities gathering together as our physical bodies.

Passing through all of those lives, we've created karma at every stage. We've created karma at the level of bugs, at the level of animals, at the level of birds, and again at the level of human beings. All of this karma appears one after another, bringing with it all kinds of hardships and suffering. It comes out according to circumstance, sometimes appearing as if it was your own thoughts, and sometimes bringing outside things to you.

Turning Dirt into Gold

All of this karma forms such a huge mountain that sometimes it just pops out at random. If we let ourselves be fooled by this karma and get caught up in it, we'll just make our lives harder. A few of you may have heard of the Snake-pit Hell or the Hell of Darkness, right? Well, if we live at the level of a snake, we'll end up being reborn in a snake's den. If we live at the level of a worm, we'll end up living in the darkness underground.

How to Escape from Hell

Let's look at how our Juingong, our inherent essence [touches her chest,] can take care of these problems. The unenlightened beings within us exist in a realm of distinctions and divisions between "me" and "you," and they bring these distinctions with them when they manifest into the world.

But if they are entrusted to this fundamental mind where there is no discrimination between "me" and "others" – to put it another way, if they awaken to the freedom of letting go of discriminations – then they will come back out into this world with a new perspective.

This is what we're learning to do. So, although we've created a mountain of karma of every kind, whatever we entrust it to this foundation will all be changed and dissolved. Everything that touches this foundation will be changed. This happens to the extent that we actually, completely, entrust what's confronting us.

We've piled up this karma over eons. It's gotten to the point where we don't even notice it, and there's so much of it that it's hard to let it go all at once. Even when you try, it probably won't melt away on the first attempt. However, if you keep working at this, then, imperceptibly, all sorts of your karma will melt away and disappear.

To be perfectly frank, things like earning a good living or not, suffering from a disease, family troubles – all of these arise from your foundation, your Juingong. They are all coming from there, so don't fall for things like hiring a shaman to chase away your troubles. Just don't. Abandoning your foundation and trying to replace it with other people's ability is such an ignorant thing to do. Karmic connections stretching back far beyond your birth have gathered together and formed your body. They've gathered together and keep coming back out in every moment of this present life, producing good and bad things according to how they were created.

But don't be misled. Have faith in your foundation, this Buddha essence, and entrust it with all of those things that are coming back out. Entrust them there [thumping her chest,] as soon as they come out. Can you guess what will happen then? Once you entrust something to your foundation, it begins to change. As it changes, everything connected to it changes. Keep entrusting these unenlightened consciousnesses so that they can all be transformed into bodhisattvas.

If you've been suffering from some pain or illness, but recovered once you entrusted it to your foundation, well, that happened because, through this foundation, those underlying karmic consciousnesses were transformed into the Medicine Buddha.

These karmic consciousnesses have spent so long fighting and beating up each other, and, as a result, all of that conflict and violence becomes karma that returns to you as something evil. It returns and fills your life with troubles and worries. It agitates you, and causes you to fight with others. As you fight and struggle, scoring blows and being beaten up, this karma keeps recreating itself time after time, growing more and more severe.

But here's what I want you to know – when you let go of all of that to your foundation, when you let go of each bit as it arises, then, there at your foundation, it will be transformed into bodhisattvas. So, once you've had this experience of transforming these karmic consciousnesses, the next time something similar arises, you'll know how to transform those karmic consciousnesses into bodhisattvas.

If you keep letting go like this, day after day, then at some unknowable point, you will have transformed all of the sentient beings within you into bodhisattvas.

When they are all transformed into bodhisattvas, light will shine forth from them, and it will be said that you have the *thirty-two marks of a Buddha*.[30] To put it another way, this body, this matter that makes up our flesh, will be filled with the energy of light, of electricity, of magnetism, and more. This energy will be working as one with everything around you, so that wherever you go, you will fill other people's world with a golden light.

Further, the *thirty-two response bodies*[31] will silently manifest from within you, according to

---

30. Thirty-two marks of a Buddha: In essence, all the characteristics of a great being. Traditionally, these were the physical characteristics reputed to be associated with great beings, such as long ears, a pleasant body odor, smooth skin, and so on.

31. Thirty-two response bodies: In Buddhist texts, these are a list of thirty-two (or thirty-three) forms that the Bodhisattva of Compassion, Avalokitesvara, manifests as in order to help people. These include the form of a Buddha, a layperson, a dragon, a great sage, a milkmaid, etc.

The thirty-two response bodies are also sometimes known as the thirty-two transformation bodies of Avalokitesvara. They're described as the manifestations of Avalokitesvara as she responds with different shapes and abilities according to people's need and circumstances. But, as Daehaeng Kun Sunim explains, these are the manifestations of our own inherent nature.

your need and that of the world around you. If you're sincere and diligent enough in your practice, you'll experience this for yourself.

There are many billions of unenlightened beings within you now, so imagine if they had all been transformed into bodhisattvas. They would fill the *universe*,[32] reaching every corner, helping all the beings they encounter. Wouldn't this be wonderful?

Now think about this: When you thoroughly let go of one problem, it's as if one hell realm has crumbled away. If you can keep letting go as things arise in your life, if you keep entrusting every problem and negative thought to your foundation one by one, then it's like you've been freed from one hell realm after another. At last, all hellish states of suffering will have completely fallen away. As the karma that was creating all of that suffering disappears, your bright, inherent nature can reveal itself.

---

32. Universe: This includes all visible realms, as well as all unseen realms.

Nothing is Fixed or Unchanging

Our mind is not corporeal. It has no form, so through your mind, you can go to Busan or any place you've ever been and come back. You can do that in a split-second, right? If someone were to say, "But how will you cross the river? There's no bridge or ferry?" do you think something like that could stop your mind? Even now, you can go home and back in an instant. If there was a river in the way, would that stop you? Of course not.

So, long ago, upon hearing Shenxiu's verse,[33] the Sixth Patriarch Huineng responded,

---

33. Shenxiu (神秀大師, 606-706 C.E.): Shenxiu was the foremost disciple of the fifth patriarch of Chinese Zen, Hongren. When Hongren was seeking an official successor, he asked all the monks studying with him to write a verse expressing their understanding. Shenxiu reluctantly complied, writing his verse on a wall.

"The body is a Bodhi tree, the mind a stand that supports the mirror of enlightenment, always work to keep them clean, and do not let dust and dirt alight."

Seeing this verse and understanding that Shenxiu had not yet awakened, Huineng replied and was chosen as Hongren's successor and the sixth patriarch.

There is no stand,
so how could there be a mirror?
Inherently, even the mirror doesn't exist,
so where could dust or dirt alight?

Like this, our fundamental mind is where everyone and everything works together as one, encompassing all times and places.

Thus, its ability is truly boundless and unimaginable. And because it's working together with everything, there's no separate thing that can be held up and labeled "fundamental mind." With a wise thought entrusted to your foundation, you can take on anything in the world. Yet a single thought lacking in wisdom can also cause us to fall into a deep pit. When you awaken to how this works and can gather everything together in your fundamental mind, becoming one with it all, you can overcome any problem in the world. Then you'll be getting close to becoming a truly worthy person, a deeply free person, and perhaps even a Buddha.

When your fundamental mind remains still, it is Buddha. When a thought is completely entrusted to it, and comes back out again, this is what was called the Dharma body. When that thought goes out and functions in the world, taking on whatever form is needed, this is what people called the transformation body of the Buddha. Functioning like this across both the seen and unseen realms is the middle way of the bodhisattvas.

So be careful to not view bodhisattvas or Buddhas as if they were beings separate from you. If you experiment with what I've been telling you today about your thoughts and foundation, and work at putting it into practice in your daily life, then regardless of what you do for a living, you can take care of everything wisely and harmoniously, and will experience a sense of the real worth of life.

As I said before, the way to dissolve karma is by completely entrusting everything to your foundation. It's this letting go and entrusting that will allow you to get a taste of who you truly are. Your true nature, your true self, is the source of everything, including your karma, so if you don't truly know your own root, you won't be able to truly understand other people, nor will you be able to understand the things you face. If you don't truly see what's underlying the situations and behaviors you're facing, your reactions and responses will be off the mark and every step forward will be a struggle.

The workings of this unseen realm of mind give rise to everything in the material realm, and everything in the material realm returns to the unseen realm. This can be called the *"one thought*[34] *from the mind that leaves no traces."*

Although I repeat myself, it's because you really have to know how the mind works. So don't blame me! [Laughs.]

---

34. One thought: This refers to the ability to raise and then input and entrust a thought to our foundation. When we can connect with our foundation like this, then through our foundation, that thought spreads to everything in the universe, including all of the lives in our body. At that instant, because all things are fundamentally not two, they all respond to that thought.

Turning Dirt into Gold 89

Everyone! Take what I'm saying today and keep engraving it in your heart. Master it so completely that I won't need to talk about this again. If I only told you pleasant or entertaining things, well, I'd be treating you badly. You need to work at this to the extent that you can deeply sense how a thought arises through your fundamental mind and then manifests into the world. When you work at this, when you apply it to the things that arise in your life and experience the results for yourself, your life will become more and more fulfilling. As you experience and play with this, any sense of futility or pointlessness will disappear.

I've heard people say that the karma we're born with is our fate, and there's nothing we can do about it. But they say this because they don't know about their fundamental mind or understand how it works. If you react outwardly when something arises, or get caught up in the outward aspect, this is you holding even tighter to that karma, so you won't be able to smooth it out or melt it down.

Instead, take whatever arises from the outside or even the inside and let it go to your foundation, Juingong. Then, as you let go of those one after another, your karma will crumble away. As every kind of suffering, as every kind of hellish state begins to fade away, your fundamental mind will begin to reveal itself, like a sprout pushing up through the earth.

As you keep doing this, your wisdom begins to arise and you'll stop blaming others for the things you experience. You'll go forward silently, taking care of whatever arises. When you take action like this, you're working from your foundation, so your actions and intentions reverberate around the world. When you speak, you speak from your foundation, and so your words carry deep wisdom. This is why it's said that a single sentence, even a single word from a true practitioner becomes the law. It manifests into the world and becomes reality.

It's often the case that when people ask me if something or someone is good or bad, they don't like my answer. "She never gives a clear answer. It's always something vague that's neither one thing nor the other."

However, if someone does something bad, and I think, "He's a bad person," it becomes much harder for him to improve. This is why I won't say he's bad or good. So, even if he were to commit a robbery right in front of me, I wouldn't say that he's a thief, or that he's not a thief.

Years ago, I met someone who was evil up to his very eyeballs, and the thought arose within me that everyone would be better off if he was dead. And surprisingly, he died almost immediately.

Whether you believe this or not, you need to know that each one of you has the ability to move the entire universe with a single thought, a single word. I can clearly see how our minds work and have experienced just how scary the functioning of mind can be. So how could I say he is "good" or "bad," as if that were some definite, unchanging fact?

If I were to say something like that, if other people were to think that, and even worse, if he himself were to think like that, then all of that energy would just push him further in that direction. It would cause him to be stuck at that level even after he dies, and the suffering that comes from existing at that level will follow him into his next life as well.

Imagine if you said something and it came true. Think about how intimidating that would be. So how can I flatly say "This is right" or "This is wrong"? You're all well aware that someone who used to do bad things can become a good person, and that someone who used to do good things can become a bad person. It's not as if people are always good or always bad. They can change in a split-second. Even someone who has consistently done bad things can reach a point where they suddenly think, "I shouldn't be doing this," and then change their direction.

Should we take people who are capable of such dramatic change and define them as bad people? I can't. As someone who understands how our fundamental mind works, I can't. As someone tasked with helping others find their path, I can't.

As someone is trying to convey the wonderful and magnificent teachings of the Buddha, I can't. You may not believe it, but the power of what happens when you entrust a thought to your fundamental mind is more than a little frightening.

This great hand of one mind! If you awaken to the wondrous principle of mind, then with a single finger you can move the entire universe! In an instant you can reach to the very depths of the universe and take care of anything! The ability to do this is no further away than the thickness of a single sheet of paper. Yet for most people, it's easier to cross the Himalayas than it is to push through that one piece of paper. It's because you haven't yet fully recognized how your mind works.

The very first step is to truly know yourself. To do this, start by trusting your foundation and turning over everything you face to it. As you keep doing this, you'll discover that the long and arduous hardships that have weighed you down are only the thickness of a single sheet of paper away from being solved.

If you can punch through this one sheet of blank paper, you can become a truly worthy person, capable of bringing about the reunification of South and North Korea. You will be able to help the people of the world settle their differences and live together a bit more harmoniously. It's because of people functioning like this that the world has continued to improve.

What You Obtain from Adversity

People sometimes ask, "Why do we have to experience bad things? Would it be so terrible to have only good things?" But consider your hands. You have both long and short fingers, don't you? You need all of them to have full use of your hand! Is there anyone who says, "This finger's short, let's chop it off!" So don't be too hasty to say what's good and what's bad, what's useful and what's useless.

For example, when unjust and unfair things happen, the minds of those who want things to change begin to coalesce, and then a revolt may even arise. Although people might feel that something is bad, even if it should come to pass, we can still help guide society grow and become more harmonious.

We all have to learn this for ourselves. It's the only way. Yet, from time to time, someone still complains that I didn't tell them everything I perceived about their business situation, which ended up costing them a lot of money. "Why didn't you warn me?" they ask. But if I had told them, it would have been one problem, avoided just one time, and soon forgotten. However, if they go through all of that once, even though it's painful, and work at using their minds wisely, then they've learned something that will be useful for the rest of their lives.

Sometimes you lose money because you're cheated, but there are also times when it was your own fault, aren't there? For instance, you can end up breaking an expensive piece of equipment because you ignored the maintenance, or you can make a mistake in your marketing campaign that costs you a lot of money. But if you take those experiences and learn everything you can from them, later what you learned could profit you greatly.

This is also the way of spiritual practice: Without getting caught up in discriminations of like or dislike, take everything that comes to you as a teacher. Learn from it and apply that back to your life. Then learn again from what happens. If you can go forward like this, you will attain the ability to take care of everything in the world.

But if you just repeat other people's theories, if you just read or listen to others' opinions about the sutras, do you really know anything? Are those your own experiences? Will those have the same power to affect your life? No, of course not.

Even if the Buddha was right here sitting with us, you'd have to drink him up and move forward. You'd have to crush him to pieces and drink him up, and then go forward. What do I mean by this? Have deep faith in your fundamental mind and entrust it with everything you experience. Keep doing this until you are able to send forth the energy of your fundamental mind. The Buddha within can take everything in and can send it out without even moving your body.

Not only does the Buddha exist within you, but all Buddhas, all bodhisattvas, absolutely everything exists within you. Because they do not exist anywhere else, Seon masters have said things like "Swallow all the water in the ocean," and "Now, that you've swallowed it, spit it back out." Or "Enter one mind," "Enter Juingong," or "Crush everything."

By the way, "Crush everything" doesn't mean to go smash something. It means becoming one with others through this non-dual, formless, fundamental mind. When this mind combines with something, there is only one. In the midst of this oneness, could anyone's mind exist apart? No.

However, because the level of each person's mind is different, there are people who get dragged around by outward things, and there are also people who do well at letting go, people who return everything inwardly. Just as energy and matter aren't separate, within this foundation of ours every kind of person and every kind of thing are all not two. So, if you let go of everything to your foundation, you will realize that you have all the power of this inherently complete mind. You will be able to apply the incredible power of our fundamental mind to everything around you. Then, in the midst of everything working together as one, if you smile and take even a single step, it will reverberate through the entire Dharma realm.

The Power of Your Inherent Essence, and Living the Good Life

I can see that some of you are thinking "I'm sick of always hearing about the same old thing," but even though you've heard this before, don't brush it off. I'm not giving these Dharma talks so that I can be popular or respected. I'm giving them to help you all. Even if I repeat something ten times, keep paying attention. You've eaten more than ten times, right? You ate breakfast, you'll have lunch, and then you'll eat dinner, won't you? You keep eating. If you skip a meal, you usually have more at the next one, don't you?

If you've known hunger, then when someone sets a full table of rice and side dishes, you'll dive into all of it. Yet, on the other hand, if you've had easy days and good food, then even at a feast, you'll only nibble on a few things. People are likewise very different in what they take away, and in how much they absorb from my Dharma talks.

Just like you eat food every day to nourish yourself, if you listen regularly to the things I've been telling you, then because you already have this inherent Buddha-nature that's the source of everything, at some point you'll suddenly understand what I've been saying. You'll know who you are and how you've come to this point. You'll know Buddha inside and out, and you'll know all other people as well. Everything about the past, present, and future is right there within your fundamental Buddha-nature.

Years ago, a man came to me saying "Sunim, my deceased parents had a hard life and suffered so much. I'm kind of poor myself, but for the last year and a half, I've been trying to save up money for a *Cheondo ceremony*.[35] But even in all this time I haven't been able to save anything." He was fighting back tears, and too choked up to speak further.

I said, "Look! If you don't have enough, just do the Cheondo ceremony without money. Why are you so worried? All of this extra worrying is just making you suffer. Anyway, would you like me to take care of this for you? Will you trust me if I say that I will guide your parents to a bright path?" He replied with a very firm, "Yes!" And in that instant his parents were taken care of. I told him, "Go home, and know that your parents will be fine."

---

35. Cheondo ceremony (薦度齋)**:** This is a ceremony to help the dead move forward on their own path of growth. More than just a memorial ceremony, its goal is to help them become unstuck and move forward at the spiritual level they attained in life, versus their state at the moment of death.

Turning Dirt into Gold

Everyone, please listen carefully, and reflect on this: The thirty-two response bodies of a Buddha all exist within you, and if your heart is very sincere, they will manifest from your foundation, responding instantly to whatever you are confronting, without leaving any trace of their coming or going. This is possible because your Buddha-nature has the inherent ability to bring in and send out every kind of energy while responding to whatever is in front of you. Without giving everything over to this Buddha-nature of yours, you won't be able to dissolve the hard suffering that comes your way. Nor will you be able to avoid getting caught up in and misled by your karma as it shows up in your life with every kind of different form.

Some people hear this story about that man and assume, "Kun Sunim directly took care of his parents," but that's not it. He was so sincere, and so desperate that his mind and my mind met, combined, and in the light that arose from that, in that instant, his parents became unstuck and were able to move forward on their own path. Please think deeply about this. If you are able to utterly let go like this, then even the sufferings of hell will collapse.

If you work at entrusting everything to your foundation, things will only improve. Even if it's just an extra pair of tongs for handling charcoal briquettes,[36] things will only improve. You won't see the least loss. So are we practicing to get rich? No, of course not. But because we're letting go of our karma bit by bit, as it melts down and disappears, our suffering and agony likewise gradually disappears, and our health, our family situation, and daily life also improve. It happens like day follows night. I know a lot of you have already had a taste of this.

---

36. These tongs were about 50 cm long, used for lifting out hot, burned up charcoal briquettes from the stoves and hot water heaters used in Korean houses. Every household had a pair, but they were often old and beat up, so no one minded getting a clean, new pair.

Let me say again, if you don't work at entrusting everything to your fundamental essence, you won't be able to dissolve your karma, nor will you be able to vanquish your suffering.

You've heard me speak of a smelting furnace before, haven't you? Whatever kind of metal gets thrown in there is melted down. No matter what form it has, no matter how dirty or rusted it is, it's all melted down and turned into shiny new metal that can become something else. It can now take a new form. When, from within this one body, the different lives inside you give rise to anger or resentment, entrust these feelings, one by one, to your fundamental mind. Then it's like you're dropping old, beat up metal into a blast furnace.

If you take these unenlightened consciousnesses that have formed from your own karma, and entrust them to your foundation, then they will be melted down and transformed into bodhisattvas. These bodhisattvas will take care of you, both inside and out, and take care of your family, your relatives, and even your ancestors.

It is so wonderful when you understand how your fundamental mind works! So how could you spend your time here at the temple play acting and praying (outwardly) to the Buddha statue for this or that? How could you forget about your inherent light? How could you ignore this, and hope that something outside yourself will bless you? How could something like an amulet be more powerful than your own Buddha-nature? Once in a while, someone says that an amulet prevented something bad, but it wasn't the amulet that did it.

Long ago, an awakened sunim happened to be passing through a village that was suffering a terrible epidemic, with people dying left and right. From a state of deep oneness with everything, he wrote out his whole-hearted wish for their well-being on a scrap of paper. He didn't have any ink, so he bit the tip of his finger and wrote it using his blood. He stuck this profound prayer on a large tree at the village's entrance and went on his way.

Soon, the epidemic stopped and the village became a very healthy place to live. That year's harvest was the best in decades, and they were completely free of outside troubles or disasters. But from then on, the villagers became obsessed with this style of talisman, always writing them and looking for new ones. They completely misunderstood what the sunim had done. It wasn't the piece of paper that helped them, but rather the energy of that sunim's fundamental mind.

If I point at a light with my finger, should you be staring at my finger? No. Look at where my finger is pointing. Like this, the amulet or talisman isn't the important element. Yet people spend their money on these, putting them in their pillow, or their mattress, or carrying them around in their pocket or purse. But all of that is useless. Why should you waste your hard-earned money on such stupid things? Carrying those around won't do a single thing to solve your problems!

When I was very little, I would go to temples a lot, but it wasn't from any kind of spiritual feelings. My father was always angry and hard on me, so I'd go there to hide from him. At home, if he saw me on my hands and knees wiping the floor with a damp cloth,[37] he'd smack me on the back and shout, "Why are you crawling?" It was so hard to endure. I'd run away just hearing the sound of his footsteps or his cough. I'd go to the temple or deep into the forest where he couldn't find me.

One day, the thought arose, "Instead of thinking of him as my father, it would be better to take the father within me as my true father." All I knew was that there was something great and warm within me. I didn't know anything about "true nature," or the incredible potential there. But in that moment, the father had found the child, and the child had found the father.[38] When they finally met, I was so incredibly happy. I wish I could describe it to you…. Let me give you a poem instead:

---

37. This is the traditional way of cleaning a heated Korean floor.

38. Here, "father" refers to our inherent nature, and "child" means our present consciousness.

*Hitting the ground and looking up at the sky,
causing the pillar of fire to rotate and support
the heavens.
This lion's[39] flame penetrates everything in the universe.
If you can freely go back and forth
between the non-material and material realms,
between the seen and unseen realms,
then every instant of your life will be upright
and magnificent.*

What do you think? Did you get some sense of how I felt? I cried so much. I didn't have the words for it back then, but this pretty much describes how I felt.

Some people can paint, others have wonderful handwriting, but I couldn't do either very well, because I'd only had a bit of elementary schooling

---

39. "Lion" refers to one who has awakened and utterly freed themselves from thoughts of an independently existing "me" or "I."

over the years.[40] So, one day, I picked up a piece of charcoal, touched it to the ground, and thought, "If you exist, write something. Writing isn't something a hand does, nor is it something only those who have gone to school can do. So, if you truly exist, do it." I sat like that for half an hour, then an hour, but my hand didn't move. Still, I didn't back down.

Back then, if I wanted to understand something or had some question that had arisen from within me, I'd easily spend the entire day staring down at the river that flowed by our neighborhood. I wouldn't move until I understood it.

Part of the reason I was so stubborn is that I wasn't afraid of anything. I'd been told "You have to die in order to see your true self," and, not

---

40. In those days, the regular schools were controlled by the Japanese government. The Korean language was forbidden, and students were forced to learn in Japanese. Many families instead sent their children to illegal, "floating" Korean schools for short periods of time. Because of their illegal nature, they would only operate for a short period of time before having to close and move to a different area.

knowing better, I took that literally. Dying didn't seem like a big deal to me. Once we're born into this world, every footstep is taking us towards death, so whether it happened sooner or a tiny bit later didn't really matter to me. Of course, now I know that life and death aren't separate, and that "dying" didn't mean the death of my flesh, but back then I didn't know any better.

So anyway, as I sat there with the charcoal in my hand and the time passing, suddenly my hand began to move quickly, writing beautiful lines of calligraphy on the ground. I'll bet you haven't experienced anything like that! [Laughs.] I'm talking about this because you should try to practice with this kind of tenacity, without any kind of "back down" in you. If you practice like this, eventually you'll know that what you think of as "life" has never existed, so death, too, does not exist.

Once in a while, poems like the one you just heard will arise within me spontaneously. I'll recite them once or twice, and that's it. I don't try to write them down or polish them. So my language may seem clunky or unsophisticated, or I may use unusual expressions, and so people miss my point. But that's how it's arising from my foundation. In your lives too, when things don't seem to be working out, when you've handled something badly, remember that the entire situation and all of those feelings arose from your foundation, and entrust them all there. Let go of even the impulse to blame yourself, and move forward.

Quietly, Even for Just Twenty Minutes at Night

When you've been working all day long and have been busy until the kids went to bed, don't get caught up in blaming yourself for forgetting about Juingong during the day. Mornings and evenings are not two separate things. They're both this present instant. In this great, transcendental mind of ours, there is no morning, no evening, no here or there, no minutes and no hours. It's all one instant; all times and places are included.

So just keep letting go of everything to your Juingong, even the thought that you've forgotten about your Juingong. Let go, too, of any thoughts that you did a good job of remembering about your Juingong. If you're trying to sit in meditation but feel too sleepy to continue, and worry that there's no hope for you to awaken, let go of that as well. Sleeping when you're tired is also a part of being in touch with your true nature.

Don't get caught up in your fixed views. Even though you feel sleepy, Juingong is the one doing that. When you feel like you need to go work on something, that's also your Juingong. Standing, sitting, walking, resting – Juingong is doing all of that. The people you meet in your life, too, are the workings of Juingong, your true nature. It's always there with you. So don't get bogged down in trivial, petty things. Just take hold of your compass, find your direction, and get moving.

Just be careful not to cause trouble for others. Be aware of how your actions will affect your family and your children. With this in the back of your mind, all you have to do is steer well. Then, you'll be headed in the right direction, and everyone will benefit from your actions, including yourself.

Once in a while I tell people this: When it's quiet at night, fight for your life, even if it's only for 20 or 30 minutes. This isn't with your fists or feet, it's taking every single thing and putting it in your foundation. Life, death, work, big things, small things, good things, bad things, trivial things, whatever. Take them all and drop them into your foundation.

It encompasses everything! [She draws a large circle in the air with her hand.] Experience what happens when you let go of all your discriminations. If you've fought to unconditionally entrust everything like this, then all confusion and harmful thoughts will disappear. In this one whole, parents and children, Buddhas and unenlightened beings, insects and the four elements are all one harmonious whole. So how could helpful and healthy solutions not arise?

Calmly, from the bottom of your heart, speak to your foundation, "Okay, Juingong. You're the only one who knows. You alone know all that I went through to evolve this far, and you're the only one who knows the path forward. I need to know you!" Keep focusing on this and entrusting it like your life depends on it. Without repeatedly struggling like this, how could you pass through that single sheet of paper that separates awakening from the fog of *ignorance*?[41]

You may think that this paper-thin difference is no big deal, and you can do it whenever you want, but do you have any idea how hard it is? There's nothing as hard as passing through this single sheet of paper. To put it another way, the only way you can do this is by making a habit of entrusting every single thing to your foundation, calmly and purposefully. Whatever you do, do it from your foundation, and do it calmly, entrusting everything

---

41. Ignorance (無明)**:** In Buddhism, "ignorance" literally means darkness. It is the unenlightened mind that does not see the truth. It is being unaware of the inherent oneness of all things, and it is the fundamental cause of birth, aging, sickness, and death.

and observing. Even when you say something, do it calmly, from your foundation.

Once Spring Arrives, Flowers Will Bloom

It's been a long talk, so let me talk about just one more thing, and then we'll move on to questions.

Long ago there was a Buddhist master who was rumored to be deeply enlightened. As he was walking through a forest, he came across a gang of bandits who were blocking the trail. One of them stood up and, drawing a long sword from across his back, began shouting and pointing with it, "Hey! I know that guy! He's supposed to be some great monk. Hey, you! Monk! They say you're some great monk with all kinds of woo-woo powers! How about I cut you open and see what's in there?!"

But the master didn't even flinch and kept walking towards the bandits. The guy with the sword, who happened to be their leader, gave a laugh, "Ha! What the hell does he know? He can't even see that he's about to die!"

All the bandits laughed as the head bandit raised his sword point and held it to the monk's chest. "Why don't we see if you can stop this sword from sliding through your chest?" The bandits were grinning and looking forward to a little blood.

Instead, the Buddhist master just chuckled, "If you hack down an old tree on the edge of winter, are you going to find a flower in there?" The bandit just stared at him.

The master repeated, "Have you ever found flowers inside a tree you've cut down?" Then, so only the bandit leader could hear, the master quietly said, "When spring comes to your mind, flowers will bloom naturally."

The bandit was stunned by those words, and at last threw down his sword and bowed low to the master. Spring really had come to his mind, and the fragrance filled the air. When the master finally continued on, the bandit and all his gang had become his disciples.

If a robber breaks into your home, if someone threatens you, it's easy to panic and start yelling and screaming. However, if you've been working at relying upon your fundamental mind, then you can calmly respond to whatever is going on.

When you're thoroughly entrusting everything like this, such that the lives within you are working together as one, then those lives will be transformed into bodhisattvas. Reaching out and connecting with whoever's in front of you, they become one with that person. And then spring comes to that person's mind, and they have no desire to hurt anyone. This is why the bandit threw down his sword.

Through this practice, you all can have the ability to cause spring to blossom within others. In an instant! The story of the awakened master exemplifies the true potential of a fully awakened mind. But this ability inherent within us all can be applied across our daily life, to all kinds of situations.

For example, suppose someone borrowed money from you and refuses to pay it back even though they have the money. In that case, don't get angry, and don't badmouth him. Instead, with a kind heart, entrust the whole situation to your foundation, along with the intention that things go well for him and he's at peace. Then, if he's in a good place, it's likely his attitude will change, and he'll pay back the money he owes.

If you want to master something, whether it's martial arts, music, or anything else, you have to focus directly on that and not let yourself be distracted by other things. Understand? If you stay focused on entrusting everything to your foundation, then eventually you'll know what it means to be truly free.

I expect that everyone here has had experiences and situations that you've had a hard time practicing with, where you couldn't quite figure out what was going on or how to handle it. Right? So, today, go ahead and ask me about those, without being embarrassed or worried about what others might think.

Isn't Worrying about Money a Form of Greed?

Questioner 1 (Male) I'd like to ask you about the problem of money. It's one of the most worldly things, yet something that causes people more stress and worry than almost anything else.

People need money to get by and put a lot of effort into earning it. It's almost impossible to live without it. We can't ignore it, yet in Buddhism we are warned about the Three Poisons of greed, anger, and ignorance. I've thought about this for a while now, and I can't help but think that all of this concern for money and even the wish to be better off are just manifestations of greed and covetousness.

Sometimes the deep wish to earn more money almost feels like a prayer touched by something holy, yet at other times it just feels like covetousness. When I step back and look at this greed, I have to ask myself whether I actually believe in Buddhism. And sometimes the people around me say the same thing. Could you please help me understand this?

Kun Sunim   While living in this world, if we don't have money, things can get rather stressful, can't they? [Chuckles.] But when you truly need money, there's a method that will ensure what you need shows up, without obsessing over piling up money or trying to borrow it from others. If you just work at entrusting your worries and fears to your inherent Buddha essence, then money, minds, and bodies will all come together as one, and respond to your Buddha-nature as it takes care of what's facing you.

For example, if you want to make kimchi for an elderly neighbor but don't have any large containers, then, if you've been entrusting that, your foundation knows about it. "Aha, she needs containers if she's going to run my errand." It arranges for you to get the containers you need. It's exactly the same for money. If you're always worried and restless about getting money or paying it back, then it's as if money peeks into your house, see what's going on, and runs away as fast as possible. Money looks in, sees the chaos, and thinks, "If I go in this house, everyone will be shouting and fighting over me, and I'll get ripped to pieces."

So entrust everything to your true doer, your Juingong. If you need something, make this foundation bring it to you. If you try to force something, whether it's money or anything else, if you try to scheme and use your will to pull it towards you, it won't stick around. Even when your efforts seem to work, it will leave before too long. Within the hour, that money, or whatever, will be trying to leave. It may be with you for a week or a year, but when it leaves, it will take the same amount with it, plus interest.

Years ago, before we built this Dharma Hall, we didn't have any money. Just nothing! And yet we built this very solid, four-story building almost overnight. It wasn't due to a few rich donors, but rather because many people gathered together and raised the intention that we should have a Dharma Hall. They collected small amounts from everyone, and we finished construction before too long.

Turning Dirt into Gold

But if I'd been trying to do all this from some sense of grasping, or thinking that it was "my" temple, then it wouldn't have happened. This is everyone's Dharma Hall, so we were able to build it. Even when your desire for money isn't coming from greed, you still shouldn't get caught up in praying for money or wealth.

Think about life in Korea during the old days. Well, our situation is bit like that, where our true nature is the master of the house, and our present consciousness is the servant. All the servant has to do is run errands for the master. If there's no money in the house, that's the master's problem, not the servant's. The master is already well aware of whether there's enough money or not. He's already working to take care of that and will naturally take care of the servants. If he gives you more money, great. If he doesn't, then you just go on.

You need to have this kind of attitude. If you keep living like this, later you will be able to become one with this true master, living freely in the truest sense. At this point, there will be no master and no servant.

So don't try to come up with schemes for making money. Don't go around full of thoughts about money, and don't have your fingers wrapped around your money. People who go around clinging to money are always losing it, while people who let go of thoughts of money, well, they never run out of money, even after a thousand years.

Why? Because all money is theirs. If you try to pile up money, thieves will get a scent of it and come looking. Even if you don't carry around money, when you need it, money will come to you. It may be that someone just gives it to you. If you use that money wisely, that will also create *virtue and merit*[42] for the person who gave it to you.

---

42. Virtue and merit (功德): Here this term refers to the results of helping people or beings unconditionally and non-dually, without any thought of self or other. It becomes virtue and merit when you "do without doing," that is, doing something without the thought that "I did such and such." Because it is done unconditionally, all beings benefit from it.

Don't let yourself become overly worried about money. Instead, work on trusting your foundation. If you're working on communicating and connecting with this inner foundation, then once it realizes something is lacking, it will work to bring that to you. It's this foundation that has formed you, it's this foundation that moves you and enables you to live, so have faith in it and trust it with everything you're going through.

Cut-throat Competition and Spiritual Practice

Questioner 2 (Male) I am very pleased to be here and have a chance to ask you questions. My question is about practicing Buddhist teachings in the workplace.

I'm a professor at a university and I believe that every part of our daily life exists within the truth the Buddha talked about. So we should be able to live our lives in accord with this, but I've had some problems applying these teachings at work. Actually, what you've taught us seems much more helpful in dealing with my family and home life. But at work, where everything depends upon so many other people, the teachings seem to create problems.

It seems to me that at work, people are evaluated by the logic of economics and competition, with people trying to get as much as they can for the least effort. All the while, they're trying to outdo and defeat everyone else. It seems like you have to do both in order to be recognized.

However, as I've tried to let go of my attachment to winning and succeeding, people I work with have started saying that I've become lazy after I started going to the temple. So I would like to know how I should handle this.

Kun Sunim That happened because you haven't behaved wisely. You've mistaken "taking it easy" for "relying upon my foundation."

Questioner 2 What I meant was that employees everywhere get evaluated and graded and judged based on those things. It seems to me that in order to get a promotion, you have to figure out how to get as much credit as possible regardless of your actual work, and you have to cut down the people above you in order to advance. But what you teach doesn't seem to….

Kun Sunim Whether you're awarded a high position, or recognized by others, isn't up to you. That's up to your foundation, your true doer. Think about how you reach out to shake hands with someone you're happy to see. The mind that's happy to see them is there first, and then your hand just moves. You don't try to calculate your movements, you just do it.

Everything is inherently like this; your body follows the direction of your mind. It just flows afterward. It's not "me" doing it. And it absolutely doesn't mean that you ignore what needs doing. You take care of what needs to be done, but you do so while letting go of thoughts of "me" and "I'm doing." This is the only thing you need to worry about. It's your foundation that moves first, and then everything else follows accordingly. Do you have any other questions?

Questioner 2   It seems to me that we need to work hard at spiritual practice so we can create a great Seon center that can help train the leaders of the country. However, Anyang [where this Dharma talk was taking place] is on the outskirts of Seoul, and this location seems a bit remote to do that. This doesn't really bother me, but I think that if the center was in the middle of Seoul, then important people, maybe even the president, would come here and learn, and that would be good for the country.

Kun Sunim [Sighs.] That's something that depends upon people's ability and readiness for spiritual practice. Most people these days approach Buddhism through classes and books. And even among sunims, there aren't very many who learn through meditation and application. Still fewer practice entrusting everything to their true nature, knowing, "You're the one who has to reveal yourself." Instead, most just sit reflecting on old *hwadus*.[43] On other people's hwadus.

Even the word "Seon" is just a label. What you have to do is know yourself. You have to learn to believe in yourself. You have to learn to rely upon your inherent Buddha-nature! Spiritual practice isn't about looking for something that you don't have, it's about learning to rely upon your inherent foundation.

This inherent foundation of yours has no form. Because it has no form, it isn't hindered by anything. Because it doesn't get caught by anything, it never gets skewed towards one side or the other, and so it always works fairly, without bias. It treats others fairly and does no harm to them, and it treats you fairly and doesn't let you lose your means of

---

43. Hwadu (話頭, C. hua-tou, J. koan)**:** Traditionally, the key phrase of an episode from the life of an ancient master, which was used for awakening practitioners, and which could not be understood intellectually. This developed into a formal training system using several hundred of the traditional 1,700 hwadus.

However, hwadus are also fundamental questions arising from inside that we have to resolve. It has been said that our life itself is the very first hwadu that we must solve.

livelihood. So entrust everything to this foundation and have faith that it will treat you fairly.

Likewise, if there's one employee in a company who practices like this, then that company will also do well. Because of one wise person, everyone else there can earn a living. A company that was in the red will start turning a profit, and even begin growing again. So wouldn't it be nice to be such a blessing to everyone around you? Wouldn't it be nice to be able to help so many people?

Spiritual practice isn't just about you and your life. It's based upon the truth that all beings are working and living together as one. Although you can't see this connection with your eyes, and even though you don't yet have the wisdom that comes from knowing this for yourself, have faith in this foundation of yours, and entrust it with everything. Trust your foundation, your Buddha-nature. Entrust it with everything you're going through. Entrust it with your hopes, feelings, and emotions. Entrust it with your worries, job, and family. Know that this foundation is your true lifeline. Only then, can you truly do the work you are here for.

Shaking hands with someone shows us that mind and intention moves first, and then the body moves. This flesh is the servant, the errand boy, for your mind. The acts of seeing, hearing, and moving your body are all happening because of this mind. All of it follows your mind. So just run errands for your inherent Buddha-nature, and let this unseen essence take care of making sure that things work out fairly.

All of this is very difficult to describe in words. Because I can't show you the actual functioning of this one mind, all that's left for me to talk about is the surface aspect — the crust and rinds, as it were. The core, well, that's up to you. That's something you'll have to taste for yourself as you experiment with this fundamental mind. My words may not be good enough, but I'll do everything I can to explain the surface workings of this fundamental mind. The important stuff, that's what you'll have to discover through application and experimentation. That's the only way you can know, feel, and taste this for yourself.

So don't get caught up in every little thing that others say about you. Don't let yourself quibble over things like employee rankings. Just remind yourself that, "Everything, including my job evaluation, my livelihood, and whether I keep or lose it, whether I'm better or worse off, that's all the working of you, my foundation." If someone keeps entrusting everything to their foundation like this, then it won't be too hard for them to experience the taste of this Buddha-nature for themselves.

This is all done in your daily life, so there's no end of opportunities. It isn't something that can only be done in sitting meditation. You can practice relying on your foundation when you're at work, when you're walking, and when you're sitting on the toilet. You can practice right where you are, as you take care of whatever needs doing. This is why it's said that sitting meditation, walking meditation, and lying-down meditation are all one. Everything can be meditation.

Questioner 2 Thank you!

The Money I Earn Comes from Everyone Working Together

Questioner 3 (Male) I came today to tell you how much of a difference your teachings have made in my life. I'm an ordinary office worker and have been with my company for 10 years or so. Years ago, I used to complain a lot about my salary. It didn't seem like much compared to the amount of work I was doing. I felt like I was working hard and wasn't getting much in return. I didn't really feel valued. At the end of the year, when I prepared my tax return, I was shocked to see how much of my salary been taken out for taxes and retirement. I complained a lot and harshly criticized our tax system.

But my feelings about this began to change after I read one of your Dharma talks where you said that, "The money you earned wasn't earned by you alone." Although my pay is still low and I wish it was a bit more, now I feel much more grateful because I see how it's the result of all my coworkers' efforts, my family, and all the people around me.

Once I began to have this sense of gratitude, my life also began to change. I became more relaxed and was able to focus on the bigger picture. I entrusted the things I undertook as well as the things I needed to this inherent foundation, Juingong, and the results have turned out really well! I keep getting surprised by just how well things turn out.

Kun Sunim Although you haven't been practicing long, I have a good feeling about you. You're exactly right about not blaming others. When people do that, nothing goes well. When people are fighting and clawing over each other, when they're trying to pin the blame on each other, then it's like money walks up to the doorway, looks in, and immediately runs away.

Money also has its own thoughts. It, too, likes peaceful places, places of laughter and joy. It, too, likes homes where people have bright hearts, where they can talk together openly about how to best use what money they have. Don't make the mistake of thinking that money is some dead material.

Money, too, wants to be useful, it wants to make a difference. It wants to be spent wisely. Money used wisely brings you blessings, but money used unwisely brings only bad karma.

That said, having a lot of money isn't necessarily a good thing. What is truly useful and good for you is having a chance to discover this foundation that we all have. So be grateful for this life we have, and make the most of it.

Cutting Off the Roots of Suffering

Questioner 4 (Male) What I'd like to ask you is why I was born into such a tough and hard life? Nothing ever really seems to get better, it's just continuously hard.

Kun Sunim As I was saying before, everything about how you lived in the past was recorded within you, and later comes back out. It's coming from you, so there's no way to avoid it. This is what each of us is living through. Here's the important point: because you were the one who created all of that, you are also the one who can solve it all. No one else has the power to do this. Being born poor or rich, being born as someone who's upright or not, confident or not, an animal or not – all of this is the result of what you've created in the past.

But what really matters is that now you can change all of it. Don't get caught up in resenting or blaming others. Although it's probably difficult, try to take whatever comes to you – no matter how hard and no matter how good – take all of that as an opportunity to change, as something to help you grow and develop.

In spite of the difficulties, if you can feel grateful towards your hardships, and entrust your foundation with everything that keeps arising, and if you can keep moving forward like this with faith, then all that you've been reinputting will change. Fate, destiny, karma, the chains of cause and effect, problems with ghosts and disease – all of this will completely disappear. What we're learning and practicing here today is the path by which we can overcome all those things.

Questioner 4 Okay, I understand. I'll try to view the hardships that come to me as materials for spiritual growth.

Kun Sunim Good. All of that truly is there to help you with your spiritual growth. Even though life can be quite hard, we have examples all around us of people who are nonetheless able to live special and praiseworthy lives.

Actually, regardless of wealth, everyone experiences so many sad and distressing things in their life. Unfortunately, the more money people get, the more arrogant they tend to become. As they become more arrogant and dissolute, their vision becomes more and more clouded. So how likely is it that they'll be well off in their next life? Not very.

What's more, any life, whether rich or poor, is actually over pretty quickly. Then it's time for a new role. Each time we're born, we receive a role suited to our spiritual ability, virtue, and merit. Sometimes that may mean we live as a rich person, and sometimes as a poor person. But that role is soon over, and we move on to something else.

All of those roles are just parts of the same whole that is this world. But when we see only the fifty percent that is the material world, these things look separate and unchanging.

If you saw the whole hundred percent, if you saw it all, you'd just laugh, saying, "It's just like flowing water! Everything is the same flowing oneness, being rich, poor, whatever! Even if I don't have any material wealth, why should I let my heart and mind be impoverished? Even life and death are part of this wholeness, so how could such words have any real importance?"

You'd sigh at all the time you had wasted not knowing this. You'd cry silent tears when you saw all the people fighting and hurting each other because they still didn't know this.

So don't worry too much about money. Instead, concern yourself with how you can live a good life in the truest sense. Further, if you work hard at helping others, and are concerned with what will truly leave them better off, then the ability to do all of this will arise from within you.

I hope that everyone here will learn about their foundation and discover the power that you each have within yourself to help everyone in the world live a good life. And I don't mean just having money or not, but the kind of life where we can see beyond just the concerns of this body. It all starts with you, so view things wisely and raise thoughts wisely.

With this, I'll finish today's Dharma talk. Thank you.

Glossary

Bodhisattva (菩薩): This usually refers to a person of great spiritual ability who is dedicated to saving those lost in ignorance and suffering. But it also means the applied energy of our fundamental nature, used to help save beings. It can also be described as the non-dual wisdom of enlightenment being used to help others awaken for themselves.

Cheondo ceremony (薦度齋): This is a ceremony to help the dead move forward on their own path of growth. More than just a memorial ceremony, its goal is to help them become unstuck and move forward at the spiritual level they attained in life, versus their state at the moment of death.

Dharma: This refers to both ultimate truth, and the truth taught by the Buddha.

Dharma realm (法界): The level of reality where everything functions as an interpenetrated and connected whole. Daehaeng Kun Sunim said that this can also be called the Dharma Net and compared it to our circulatory system, which connects and nourishes every single cell in the body.

Emptiness: Emptiness is not a void, but rather refers to the ceaseless flowing of all things. Everything is flowing as part of one whole, so there is nothing that can be separated out and set aside as if it existed independently of everything else.

There is, therefore, no "me" that exists apart from other people or other things. There is only the interpenetrated and interdependent whole, "empty" of any independent or separate selves or objects.

Fundamental mind: This refers to our inherent essence, that which we fundamentally are. "Mind," in Mahayana Buddhism, almost never means the brain or intellect. Instead it refers to this essence, through which we are inherently connected to everything, everywhere. It is intangible, beyond space and time, and has no beginning or end. It is the source of everything, and everyone is endowed with it. "Fundamental Mind" is interchangeable with other terms such as "Buddha-nature," "True nature," "True self," and "Foundation."

Hanmaum[han-ma-um]: Han means one, great, and combined, while maum means mind, as well as heart, and together they mean everything combined and connected as one.

What is called Hanmaum is intangible, unseen, and transcends time and space. It has no beginning or end, and is sometimes called our fundamental mind. It also means the mind of all beings and everything in the universe connected and working together as one. In English, we usually translate this as one mind.

Hwadu (話頭, C. hua-tou, J. koan): Traditionally, the key phrase of an episode from the life of an ancient master, which was used for awakening practitioners, and which could not be understood intellectually. This developed into a formal training system using several hundred of the traditional 1,700 hwadus.

However, hwadus are also fundamental questions arising from inside that we have to resolve. It has been said that our life itself is the very first hwadu that we must solve.

Ignorance (無明): In Buddhism, "ignorance" literally means darkness. It is the unenlightened mind that does not see the truth. It is being unaware of the inherent oneness of all things, and it is the fundamental cause of birth, aging, sickness, and death.

Juingong (主人空): Pronounced "ju-in-gong." Juin (主人) means the true doer or the master, and gong (空) means empty. Thus Juingong is our true nature, our true essence, the master within, which is always changing and manifesting, without a fixed form or shape.

Daehaeng Sunim has compared Juingong to the root of the tree. Our bodies and consciousness are like the branches and leaves, but it is the root that is the source of the tree, and it is the invisible root beneath the ground that sustains the visible tree.

Karmic affinity (因緣): The connection or attraction between people or things, due to previous karmic relationships.

Karmic consciousnesses (業識): Our thoughts, feelings, and behaviors are recorded as the consciousnesses of the lives that make up our body. These are sometimes called karmic consciousnesses, although they don't have independent awareness or volition. Sometime afterwards, these consciousnesses will come back out.

Thus we may feel happy, sad, angry, etc., without an obvious reason, or they may cause other problems to occur. The way to dissolve these consciousnesses is not to react to them when they arise, and instead to entrust them to our foundation.

However, even these consciousnesses are just temporary combinations, so we shouldn't cling to the concept of them.

Middle realm (world)**:** In Buddhism, the realm of human beings is sometimes described as the "middle realm" or the "middle world," because it is said to be one of six realms. It exists below the realms of more advanced beings, called devas and asuras, but above the realms of animals, hungry ghosts, and the various hell states.

Ocean Seal (海印)**:** This term has a number of nuances, the most common of which is having, without a doubt (as if stamped with a seal), attained the state where the functioning of everything is perceived clearly and truly, like images seen on calm water. It also includes the nuance of horizons without end and depths that cannot be measured.

One mind (Hanmaum [han-ma-um])**:** From the Korean, where "one" has a nuance of great and combined, while "mind" is more than intellect and includes "heart" as well. Together, they mean everything combined and connected as one.

What is called "one mind" is intangible, unseen, and transcends time and space. It has no beginning or end, and is sometimes called our fundamental mind. It also means the mind of all beings and everything in the universe connected and working together as one.

One thought: This refers to the ability to raise and then input and entrust a thought to our foundation. When we can connect with our foundation like this, then through our foundation, that thought spreads to everything in the universe, including all of the lives in our body. At that instant, because all things are fundamentally not two, they all respond to that thought.

Pillar of mind: Similar to Jujangja (拄杖子), which is a monk's staff, but the term is used figuratively to refer to our fundamental mind.

Prajna: Insight into the true nature of reality, namely the awareness of impermanence, emptiness, and non-self.

Returning back (回向)**:** In Korean Buddhism, this implies the practice of giving back or sharing with others at the successful conclusion of something. While it's understood that this is a good thing to do, and will also benefit oneself and one's ancestors, it doesn't have the strong nuance of "transferring merit to one's ancestors" that it has in Chinese Buddhism.

Samsara: The ceaseless cycle of birth and death that all living things are continuously passing through.

Seon (禪) (Chan, Zen)**:** Seon describes the unshakeable state where one has firm faith in their inherent foundation, their Buddha-nature, and so returns everything they encounter back to this fundamental mind. It also means letting go of "I," "me," and "mine" throughout one's daily life.

Sunim / Kun Sunim: Sunim is the respectful title of address for a Buddhist monk or nun in Korea, and Kun Sunim is the title given to outstanding nuns or monks.

Thirty-two marks of a Buddha: In essence, all the characteristics of a great being. Traditionally, these were the physical characteristics reputed to be associated with great beings, such as long ears, a pleasant body odor, smooth skin, and so on.

Thirty-two response bodies: In Buddhist texts, these are a list of thirty-two (or thirty-three) forms that the Bodhisattva of Compassion, Avalokitesvara, manifests as in order to help people. These include the form of a Buddha, a layperson, a dragon, a great sage, a milkmaid, etc.

The thirty-two response bodies are also sometimes known as the thirty-two transformation bodies of Avalokitesvara. They're described as the manifestations of Avalokitesvara as she responds with different shapes and abilities according to people's need and circumstances. But, as Daehaeng Kun Sunim explains, these are the manifestations of our own inherent nature.

Universe: This includes all visible realms, as well as all unseen realms

Virtue and merit (功德): Here this term refers to the results of helping people or beings unconditionally and non-dually, without any thought of self or other. It becomes virtue and merit when you "do without doing," that is, doing something without the thought that "I did such and such." Because it is done unconditionally, all beings benefit from it.

Other Books by Seon Master Daehaeng

English
- Wake Up And Laugh (Wisdom Publications)
- No River To Cross (Wisdom Publications)
- My Heart Is A Golden Buddha (Hanmaum Publications)
  Also available as an audiobook
- Standing Again (Hanmaum Publications)
- Sharing The Same Heart (Hanmaum Publications)
- Touching The Earth (Hanmaum Publications)
- A Thousand Hands Of Compassion
  (Hanmaum Publications) [Korean/English]
- One Mind: Principles (Hanmaum Publications)
  *All of these are available in paper or ebook formats

- Practice in Daily Life (Korean/English bilingual series)
  1. To Discover Your True Self, "I" Must Die
  2. Walking Without A Trace
  3. Let Go And Observe
  4. Mind, Treasure House Of Happiness
  5. The Furnace Within Yourself
  6. The Spark That Can Save The Universe
  7. The Infinite Power Of One Mind
  8. In The Heart Of A Moment
  9. One With The Universe
  10. Protecting The Earth
  11. Inherent Connections
  12. Finding A Way Forward
  13. Faith In Action
  14. The Healing Power Of Our Inner Light
  15. The Doctor Is In
  16. Turning Dirt into Gold
  17. Dancing On the Whirlwind

Korean
- 건널 강이 어디 있으랴 (Hanmaum Publications)
- 내 마음은 금부처 (Hanmaum Publications)
- 처음 시작하는 마음공부1 (Hanmaum Publications)

Russian
• Дзэн И Просветление (Amrita-Rus)

German
• Wache Auf und Lache (Theseus)
• Umarmt von Mitgefühl (Deutsch-Koreanisch, Diederichs)
• Wie fließendes Wasser (Goldmann)
• Wie fließendes Wasser - CD (steinbach sprechende bücher)
• Vertraue und lass alles los (Goldmann)
• Grundlagen (Hanmaum Publications, New)

Czech
• Probuď se! (Eugenika)

Spanish
• Ningún Río Que Cruzar (Kailas Editorial)
• Una Semilla Inherente Alimenta El Universo (Hanmaum Publications)
• Si Te Lo Propones, No Hay Imposibles (Hanmaum Publications)
• El Camino Interior (Hanmaum Publications)
• Vida De La Maestra Seon Daehaeng (Hanmaum Publications)
• Enseñanzas De La Maestra Daehaeng (Hanmaum Publications)

Indonesian
• Sup Cacing Tanah (PT Gramedia)

Vietnamese
• Không có sông nào để vượt qua
  (Hanmaum Publications; Vien Chieu, Vietnam)
• tỉnh thức và cười
  (Hanmaum Publications; Vien Chieu, Vietnam)
• Chạm mặt đất (Hanmaum Publications; Vien Chieu, Vietnam)

Chinese
• 我心是金佛（简体字）(Hanmaum Publications, 韩国)
• 无河可渡（简体字）(Hanmaum Publications, 韩国)
• 人生不是苦海（繁体字）(Hanmaum Publications, 韩国)
• 我心是金佛（繁体字）(橡树林文化出版, 台湾)

Anyang Headquarters of Hanmaum Seonwon

1282 Gyeongsu-daero, Manan-gu, Anyang-si,
Gyeonggi-do, 13908, Republic of Korea
Tel: (82-31) 470-3175 / Fax: (82-31) 470-3209
www.hanmaum.org/eng
onemind@hanmaum.org

Overseas Branches of Hanmaum Seonwon

ARGENTINA
Buenos Aires
Miró 1575, CABA, C1406CVE, Rep. Argentina
Tel: (54-11) 4921-9286 / Fax: (54-11) 4921-9286
http://hanmaumbsas.org

Tucumán
Av. Aconquija 5250, El Corte, Yerba Buena,
Tucumán, T4107CHN, Rep. Argentina
Tel: (54-381) 425-1400
www.hanmaumtuc.org

BRASIL
São Paulo
R. Newton Prado 540, Bom Retiro
Sao Paulo, CEP 01127-000, Brasil
Tel: (55-11) 3337-5291
www.hanmaumbr.org

CANADA
Toronto
20 Mobile Dr., North York, Ontario M4A 1H9, Canada
Tel: (1-416) 750-7943
www.hanmaum.org/toronto

GERMANY
Kaarst
Broicherdorf Str. 102, 41564 Kaarst, Germany
Tel: (49-2131) 969551 / Fax: (49-2131) 969552
www.hanmaum-zen.de

THAILAND
Bangkok
86/1 Soi 4 Ekamai Sukhumvit 63
Bangkok, Thailand
Tel: (66-2) 391-0091
www.hanmaum.org/cafe/thaihanmaum

USA
Chicago
7852 N. Lincoln Ave., Skokie, IL 60077, USA
Tel: (1-847) 674-0811
www.hanmaum.org/chicago

Los Angeles
1905 S. Victoria Ave., L.A., CA 90016, USA
Tel: (1-323) 766-1316
www.hanmaum.org/la

New York
144-39, 32 Ave., Flushing, NY 11354, USA
Tel: (1-718) 460-2019 / Fax: (1-718) 939-3974
www.juingong.org

Washington D.C.
7807 Trammel Rd., Annandale, VA 22003, USA
Tel: (1-703) 560-5166
www.hanmaum.org/wa

If you would like more information about these books or
would like to order copies of them,
please call or write to:

Hanmaum International Culture Institute
Hanmaum Publications
1282 Gyeongsu-daero, Manan-gu, Anyang-si,
Gyeonggi-do, 13908,
Republic of Korea
Tel: (82-31) 470-3175
Fax: (82-31) 470-3209
e-mail: onemind@hanmaum.org
www.hanmaumbooks.org